The Discourse of Child Counselling

Impact: Studies in language and society

IMPACT publishes monographs, collective volumes, and text books on topics in sociolinguistics. The scope of the series is broad, with special emphasis on areas such as language planning and language policies; language conflict and language death; language standards and language change; dialectology; diglossia; discourse studies; language and social identity (gender, ethnicity, class, ideology); and history and methods of sociolinguistics.

General Editor

Anna Deumert
Monash University

Advisory Board

Peter Auer
University of Freiburg

Jan Blommaert
Ghent University

Annick De Houwer
University of Antwerp

J. Joseph Errington
Yale University

Anna Maria Escobar
University of Illinois at Urbana

Guus Extra
Tilburg University

Marlis Hellinger
University of Frankfurt am Main

Elizabeth Lanza
University of Oslo

William Labov
University of Pennsylvania

Peter H. Nelde
Catholic University Brussels

Peter L. Patrick
University of Essex

Jeanine Treffers-Daller
University of the West of England

Victor Webb
University of Pretoria

Volume 21

The Discourse of Child Counselling
by Ian Hutchby

The Discourse
of Child Counselling

Ian Hutchby
University of Leicester

John Benjamins Publishing Company
Amsterdam/Philadelphia

The paper used in this publication meets the minimum requirements of American National Standard for Information Sciences – Permanence of Paper for Printed Library Materials, ANSI z39.48-1984.

Library of Congress Cataloging-in-Publication Data

Hutchby, Ian.
　The discourse of child counselling / by Ian Hutchby.
　　p. cm. -- (Studies in language and society, ISSN 1385-7908 ; v. 21)
　Includes bibliographical references and index.
　1. Children of divorced parents. 2. Counseling. 3. Conversation analysis. 4. Sociolinguistics. I. Title.

HQ777.5.H88 2007
362.7--dc22
　　　　　　　　　　　　　2006101276
ISBN 978 90 272 1859 9 (Hb; alk. paper)
ISBN 978 90 272 1860 5 (Pb; alk. paper)

© 2007 – John Benjamins B.V.
No part of this book may be reproduced in any form, by print, photoprint, microfilm, or any other means, without written permission from the publisher.

John Benjamins Publishing Co. · P.O. Box 36224 · 1020 ME Amsterdam · The Netherlands
John Benjamins North America · P.O. Box 27519 · Philadelphia PA 19118-0519 · USA

Table of contents

Acknowledgements — VII
Transcription conventions — IX
Supplementary note on the presentation of data — XI

CHAPTER 1
Child counselling and children's social competence — 1
   The sociology of childhood and the competence paradigm — 5
   Children's talk and social competence — 9
   Child counselling as an 'arena of action' — 13
   Outline of the book — 17

CHAPTER 2
Child counselling as institutional interaction — 19
   Conversation analysis: Origins and overview — 19
   What counts as data: Tapes and transcripts — 20
   Turn-taking: Some basic observations — 22
   Exhibiting understanding in the next turn — 25
   Adjacency pairs: The conditional relevance of next position — 27
   CA, social organisation and insitutional contexts — 30
   Institutional interaction, task-orientation and *bricolage* — 34

CHAPTER 3
'So this is being taped': From ethics to analytics in the data collection process — 39
   From ethics to analytics — 41
   Observability: 'Being recorded' — 46
   Analysability: 'Being heard' and the moral status of the technology — 50
   Conclusion — 56

CHAPTER 4
Talking about feelings: The perspective-display series in child counselling — 59
   The perspective-display series — 61
   Perspective displays in child counselling — 66
   Counselling perspectives and therapeutic vision — 74
   Conclusion — 78

CHAPTER 5
Active listening and the formulation of concerns 79
   Active listening in child counselling 80
   Formulations and the work of child counselling 82
   Unfolding therapeutic matters 90
   Formulations and the resistance to counselling talk 94
   Conclusion 98

CHAPTER 6
'I don't know': The interactional dynamics of resistance and response 101
   'I don't know' as an interactional object 103
   The child's strategy: 'Don't know' as a way of avoiding answering 106
   The counsellor's response: 'Don't know' and the modulation between playful and serious talk 113
   Conclusion 120

CHAPTER 7
Child counselling and the incitement to communicate 123
   A conversation-analytic take on the professional discourse of child counselling 124
   Child counselling and the difference between 'talking' and 'communicating' 127
   'Therapeutic vision' and the power dynamic in child counselling 131
   In conclusion: The importance of fine-grained observation 133

References 135
Index 143

Acknowledgements

This book addresses the nature of talk and social interaction in one form of child counselling: non-clinical 'helping' talk designed specifically for young children whose parents are in the process of separation or divorce. In order to analyse this child counselling discourse, it was necessary for me to record naturally-occurring sessions which were then transcribed. The whole project thus hung on the thread of children's (and their parents') consent to their counselling sessions being recorded. I am immeasurably grateful to those individuals who granted such consent—even though they must, for reasons of confidentiality, remain anonymous. Without them this book simply would not exist.

I am enormously grateful too to the child counsellors whose work, in that it represents the 'other half' of the child counselling dialogue, inevitably comes under scrutiny in these pages. My aim is not, and never has been, to assess, evaluate or criticise the techniques of the individual counsellors who agreed to allow my recording equipment into their offices. The book is not about finding out what is 'wrong' or 'right' with child counselling: it is about describing and analysing how it is done on the ground, as it were. There are many books available that purport to demonstrate to counsellors how it should be done. This book's sole aim is to reveal how it is done; how the complex work of counselling young children is accomplished amid the practical contingencies of talk-in-interaction.

The research on which the book is based was supported by the UK's major funder of social science research, the Economic and Social Research Council (ESRC). When I started work on collecting the data, I had no idea what the outcomes of the research might be; nor, indeed, was I at all certain that there would turn out to be a research project at all, given that I was entirely reliant on the agreement of young children and their (usually) estranged parents before any data could be gathered. It is gratifying, therefore, that a body as large-scale and apparently outcomes-oriented as the ESRC could demonstrate a willingness still to fund radical and 'blue sky' projects such as this one. For me, this acts as a welcome indication that those of us who work in the field of conversation analysis can still produce research that is valued by the mainstream social science organisations. This is important, for I believe that while it is easy to see this kind of research as necessarily on the margins of—or even incommensurate with—'conventional' sociology, in fact it is vital that conversation analysts convey the relevance of their studies for the range of interests at the core of the discipline.

There is one caveat that must be mentioned. This book does not aim to provide a comprehensive account of all possible types of child counselling. Like any conversation analyst, I am restricted by the data I have before me, and these were drawn from particular, and specialised, sources. Child counselling itself is a highly specialised practice currently only available in selected locations (unlike, say, psychotherapy, marriage counselling or family therapy, all of which are related yet very different concerns). The small but growing professional literature on child counselling techniques also attests to the inevitability that there exists a wide range of different ways of going about doing the work. Therefore, this book should not be read as a generic account but as a description and analysis of the nuanced practices of child counselling as observed in one particular type of setting.

Nevertheless, the issues from which I start in the following chapters—such as the incitement to communicate about feelings in situations where children are not receiving counselling at their own volition; the problem of drawing out therapeutic concerns from children's often tangential talk; or the means of responding to children's resistance to discussing therapeutic matters—are themselves generic to child counselling practice (and perhaps to counselling more generally). It is to be hoped, therefore, that my observations provide insights and resources that are useful for the varying audiences who may decide to read this book: from child counsellors themselves, to other social scientists interested in the nature of counselling discourse, to, perhaps, parents and others who may simply be interested in what kinds of things actually go on inside the child counselling office.

Ian Hutchby

Transcription conventions

Transcripts of naturally-occurring child counselling dialogues appear in these pages using the standard conventions of conversation analysis. (All names, place references and other such items have been altered to preserve anonymity.) The main aim of these symbols is to provide a sense, in written transcription, of how a stretch of talk 'sounds' on the tape. The main features foregrounded in the symbology are therefore the organisation of turns, including overlapping or interruptive talk, and features related to prosody and enunciation such as stress, emphasis, pauses, audible breathing, loudness or quietness. More detailed information on data and transcription is provided in Chapter 2. A formal account can be found in Chapter 3 of *Conversation Analysis* by Ian Hutchby and Robin Wooffitt (Polity 1998).

Glossary of transcript symbols

(0.5)   Numbers in brackets indicate a gap timed in tenths of a second.
(.)   A dot enclosed in brackets indicates a 'micropause' of less than one tenth of a second.
=   Equals signs are used to indicate 'latching' or absolutely no discernible gap between utterances; or to show the continuation of a speaker's utterance across intervening lines of transcript.
[ ]   Square brackets indicate the points where overlapping talk starts (left bracket) and ends (right bracket). Although the start of an overlap is always marked, the end is only sometimes marked.
[[Double left square brackets indicate turns that start simultaneously.
(( ))   Double brackets are used to describe a non-verbal activity: for example ((banging sound)). They are also used to enclose the transcriber's comments on contextual or other relevant features.
( )   Empty brackets indicate the presence of an unclear utterance or other sound on the tape.
.hhh   h's preceded by a dot are used to represent audible inward breathing. The more h's, the longer the breath.
hhhh   h's with no preceding dot are used in the same way to represent outward breathing.

huh heh hih	Laughter is transcribed using 'laugh tokens' which, as far as the transcriber is able, represent the individual sounds that speakers make while laughing.
sou:::nd	Colons indicate the stretching of a sound or a word. The more colons the greater the extent of the stretching.
sou-	A dash indicates a word suddenly cut-off during an utterance.
. , ?	Punctuation marks are not used grammatically, but to indicate prosodic aspects of the talk. A full stop indicates a falling tone; commas indicate fall-rise or rise-fall (i.e. a 'continuing' tone); question marks indicate a marked rising tone.
↑↓	Upward and downward arrows are used to mark an overall rise or fall in pitch across a phrase.
a:	Underlining of a letter before a colon indicates a small drop in pitch during a word.
a:	Underlining of a colon after a letter indicates a small rise in pitch at that point in the word.
Underline	Other underlining indicates speaker emphasis. Words may be underlined either in part or in full, depending on the enunciation.
CAPITALS	Capitals mark a section of speech markedly louder than that surrounding it.
→	Arrows in the left margin point to specific parts of the transcript discussed in the text.
° °	Degree signs are used to indicate that the talk between them is noticeably quieter than surrounding talk.
< >	Outward chevrons are used to indicate that the talk between them is noticeably slower than surrounding talk.
> <	Inner chevrons are used to indicate that the talk between them is noticeably quicker than surrounding talk.

Supplementary note on the presentation of data

When preparing the manuscript for this book, I gave a lot of consideration to the question of how to describe the key participants in the data—that is, child counsellors and young children—and especially how to represent them as speakers in the data extracts that are scattered throughout these pages. Should I describe and represent them simply as 'child' and 'counsellor'? Or even more neutrally, simply as 'A' and 'B'? Or should I use the anonymised names I gave them for my own records, which would at least give the reader an indication of their respective gender? Or should I use a combination of names and, for the children at least, ages?

I quickly ruled out the 'A' and 'B' option, for the simple reason that in almost any conceivable situation of talk-in-interaction, and especially in institutional settings, we do not encounter one another as anonymous 'A's and 'B's. In certain quarters there is an argument that this is, in fact, the best way of representing participants for the purpose of analysis, since it avoids imputing any a priori identity characteristics that may not accord with the identities that are relevant, moment by moment, to the participants themselves. Such a position would therefore rule out my other options. For instance, to use the terms 'Counsellor' and 'Child' or 'Counsellor, 35' and 'Child, 7' might be taken to imply that these are fixed and concrete identity categories in terms of which the participants consistently orient to one another. Yet while this would, it is true, be an incorrect assumption (many other identities can become relevant and be demonstrably oriented to in the course of interaction) it seems equally true that the participants do not simply encounter one another as anonymous entities in a blank space, like characters in a Samuel Beckett play.

Therefore, in the interests of finding some balance between these positions, I adopted the policy of referring to participants in data extracts using single letters, but ones that both (a) indicated primary identity characteristics that were relevant—oriented to—by the participants themselves (even if not in every single utterance or action) and (b) provided a small amount of interpretive information (i.e. more than would be offered by 'A' and 'B') that could be useful for the readers of my analysis. Counsellors are referred to in all data extracts as 'C'. Where it seems relevant to index their gender, that is mentioned in the text surrounding the extract. Children are referred to using the first letter of the Christian names I invented for each of them. The main names used, and their ages at the time of the recordings, are Graham (4), Ben (5), Peter (6), Jenny (8), Dan (8), Pamela (10) and Amanda (12).

Thus, the following example is an exchange between a Counsellor and the child anonymised as Peter:

1 C: Are you surprised they said you couldn't go.
2 P: Ye_ah,
3 C: You are.
4 P: Mm.

CHAPTER 1

Child counselling and children's social competence

This book explores the interactional organisation of child counselling. Its specific focus is on a type of counselling for young children experiencing family break-up: that is, parental separation or divorce. Family break-up has long existed as a social phenomenon, and its increasing prevalence in western culture has been recognised since at least the middle of the 20th century. But it is only comparatively recently that children's views about and responses to parental separation have come to be treated seriously enough to warrant investment in specialist child counselling services. Many such services now operate on a self-referral or 'walk-in' basis with offices situated in town and city high streets. Families experiencing break-up or other difficulties are invited to seek appointments simply by phoning or going along to the office. Therefore, the child counsellors working in such practices do not tend to deal with children exhibiting severe behavioural problems, who would more likely be referred to clinical psychologists, or at risk of harm, in which case the child would likely be assigned to social workers. Instead, they deal largely with children whose parents feel that some sort of help is needed in getting the child to come to terms with the decision they have made to separate. Thus, the children in this study have not been referred for counselling through a medical route but on a voluntary basis; although the volition is more usually that of the parents rather than the child—an issue which affects the counselling in certain ways as the following chapters will show.

The book is based on tape-recordings of the work of a London-based high street child counselling and family mediation practice. The counsellors had a particular way of working which involved three steps. First, children and their parent(s) were seen together in an initial assessment meeting at which the purpose and structure of the counselling was explained and any possible concerns were raised. In the second step, the child counselling itself took place. Here, importantly, children were seen on their own by the counsellor for between four and six sessions, a series which could stretch across two or three months. During these sessions, parents were required to wait in a separate room. Counsellors took no written notes during the sessions themselves (although, as described later, for the purpose of my research these sessions were tape-recorded with the participants' consent) and the content of their discussions was treated as confidential between counsellor and child. Counsellors would write up their notes after each session had ended, and these notes would then inform discussions in the third step, which was to hold a concluding meeting where parents, children and counsellors would again be present. The aim of this meeting was for counsellor and child jointly to provide parents with feedback about concerns raised and suggestions for going forward resulting from the series of one-to-one sessions.

This way of working makes child counselling very different from family therapy—another widely practised form of counselling for relational and behavioural problems in families. In family therapy, the preference is usually for counsellors to see family members of different generations together. While in certain circumstances the parents may be seen individually, or the children may be seen without their parents, much family therapy tends to adopt a 'systems' approach in which family problems are treated as emerging from the systems of interpersonal relationships and ways of communicating that characterise individual families. Thus, the solution to the difficulties which have brought the family to counselling is treated as residing in changes to the family system, and various practices are utilised to involve all family members in recognising and adopting those changes (see, for example, Boscolo et al. 1986).

By contrast, in the form of child counselling that is the subject of this book, the focus is entirely upon the child or children of the family. Indeed, in the course of my exploratory discussions about the research with practitioners, the view was often expressed that the counselling session represented 'the child's space': a confidential environment in which children were enabled to speak in whatever way they pleased without worrying about possible repercussions from their parents. This even led some counsellors to decline their participation in the study I was undertaking. For these counsellors, my request to be allowed to tape-record sessions constituted a breach of confidentiality[1] and an incursion into the child's space which they felt they could not warrant. In child counselling, therefore, a different (though possibly related) model seems to operate, in which it is felt primarily important to attain understanding of the child's own view of whether they experience any difficulties associated with their parents' separation, and if so, what those difficulties are and—perhaps most crucially—what the child him or herself feels are the most appropriate solutions to those difficulties.

As we will see, this means that child counselling discourse takes particular, and often quite unusual, forms. Counsellors appear to have fairly clear ideas about the kind of talk—or the kinds of topics—that they are aiming for. Thus, their interac-

---

1. This was so even though during the consent process confidentiality agreements were signed which ensured that neither parents nor counsellors would have access to the tapes or transcripts.

tions with children tend to be scattered with references to 'muddles' or 'jumbles'; to the child's 'anger', 'sadness' or 'confusion'; or to the child's ideas as to 'why' their parents do or say the things they do. Children, on the other hand, have a much less clear-cut sense of how to approach the talk of the counselling session. While they may be happy to talk at length about everyday affairs—the 'small talk' with which counsellors often open up sessions—they become far more taciturn when it comes to discussing family 'problems'. Indeed, children very rarely volunteer any information about their 'concerns'; and given that child counselling is, ostensibly, about addressing precisely such concerns, it falls to counsellors to find ways of trying to draw them out as the session unfolds.

In the light of these matters, then, the book can be said to address the following core analytical topics:

- The techniques by which counsellors draw out children's concerns about family trauma.
- The resources children use to make sense of their experience in the light of counsellors' questions.
- The discursive means by which children are situated as therapeutic subjects.
- The means by which children, through talking and avoiding talking, cooperate in or resist their therapeutic subjectification.

The approach I take to these topics is a sociological and linguistic one, building on the work of ethnomethodologists (Garfinkel 1967) and conversation analysts (Sacks 1992) who, since the 1960s, have encouraged social scientists to take naturally occurring dialogues as topics of analysis in their own right. In the domain of counselling research, Peräkylä (1995) and Silverman (1996) earlier adopted this approach to investigate HIV counselling for adults, showing how a close examination of talk and its organisation can provide valuable insights into the kinds of strategies used by counsellors to help clients make sense of, and find ways of dealing with, problematic or extraordinary situations. Silverman (1996) in particular was concerned to argue that such an approach should not be seen simply as a 'nit-picking' obsession with the micro-details of talk, but instead feeds into key sociological concerns with the role of institutional practices in contemporary everyday life and with the significance of discourse as a principal means of mediating social relations.

As Silverman (1996: 208) remarks, the essence of counselling is that each centre, or service, 'offers an institutionalised incitement to speak according to its own practical theories'. In order to see how that incitement to speak operates in practice, it is necessary to examine the details of actual talk produced during the course of counselling interaction. Accordingly, audio recordings of sessions were made with the consent of children (whose names and points of reference have been anonymised) and their parents. Negotiation of consent was organised during the initial assessment meetings (see Chapter 3 for further details). A series of sessions (usually the full series) was captured for each case for which consent was granted. The cases involve children ranging from 4 to 12 years old, and include sessions conducted by both male and female counsellors. Additionally, the cases include single children and siblings, both male-male and male-female. In the latter cases, there are examples of siblings seen both together and separately.

The tapes were transcribed and analyzed according to the procedures of conversation analysis, or CA (see Chapter 2). CA treats talk within social interaction both as highly socially organised, and as a means of producing social organisation (Hutchby and Wooffitt 1998). As a method, it focuses on the sequential organization of talk-in-interaction, and investigates how turn-taking is involved in the collaborative production of intersubjectivity along with other key elements of human sociality. As we see in more detail in Chapter 2, CA not only takes a distinctive perspective on the nature of talk-in-interaction as a collaboratively achieved, socially organised practice, but also on the nature of the specialised or 'institutional' settings in which a significant amount of talk takes place (Drew and Heritage 1992). Such settings range from courts of law (Atkinson and Drew 1979) to classrooms (Mehan 1979), from radio and television studios (Hutchby 1996, 2006) to doctors' surgeries (Heath 1992), and include the self-referral child counselling services that are the subject matter of this book.

Following this method, the questions I address concerning the operation of given counselling techniques or the nature of children's experiences of parental separation are all tied closely, and explicitly, to the observable production of talk during the session. Where questions of the efficacy of counselling talk arise, therefore, they do so in relation to how far the counsellor can be seen to succeed in eliciting from the child talk about their experiences of home or parental matters. Where questions arise about such experiences from the child's perspective, they do so in relation to how children mediate their experiences through talk. Where children are invited to mediate their feelings through other means such as drawing or game playing, as often recommended in the child counselling literature, my focus is on how interpretations of such materials are drawn out interactionally within the real-time unfolding of talk between counsellor and child.

Before proceeding to a more detailed account of this methodological standpoint, it is important to fill in some of the broader conceptual and theoretical background in terms of which the book should be understood. First of all I will provide a consideration of relevant developments in the sociology of childhood and the cross-disciplinary analysis of children's talk. Subsequently I will discuss related issues such as the relationship between children's social competence and institutional arenas for talk and interaction, of which child counselling is one example.

These issues are important not simply in the abstract, but because social science thinking in these areas can in fact be related to shifts in wider social understandings of children and the development of childhood policy. For example, in the UK, the Children Act of 1989 sought to place children's own viewpoints and understandings more centrally within legal considerations and medical decisions involving child welfare. This is related to other developments, on a wider international scale, in social policy concerning children; for example, the United Nations Charter on the Rights of Children (UNCRC) which seeks to prioritise children's participation in decision-making processes affecting their lives at a whole range of different levels. These legal and policy developments are related both to the movement towards understanding children's social competencies in the sociology of childhood, and to the underlying rationale for the provision of specialised child counselling services. They are thus at the core of how we can understand the nature of talk and interaction in child counselling sessions.

The sociology of childhood and the competence paradigm

During the 1990s, what has been described as a 'competence paradigm' emerged in the sociology of childhood (James and Prout 1990; Waksler 1991; Mayall 1994a; Hutchby and Moran-Ellis 1998). This paradigm is based on a critique of many of the assumptions underpinning the perspective on children and childhood put forward for much of the 20th century by certain schools of thought in developmental psychology and in sociology (Mackay 1973). The influential work of Piaget (1926) in child psychology encouraged a view of development as a set of predetermined 'stages' that children must pass through before they reach full (i.e. adult) social competence; while the equally influential work of Parsons (1951) in sociology posited 'socialisation' as an overarching psycho-social process over which children have no control and by means of which they are inculcated with the norms of full adult societal membership. As Mackay (1973: 28) puts it: 'Children are incomplete—immature, irrational, incompetent, asocial, acultural . . . . Adults, on the other hand, are complete—mature, rational, competent, social, and autonomous unless they are "acting like children".' The purpose of developmental and socialisation processes is to ensure the successful transformation of the former (children) into the latter (adults).

One consequence of this picture has been that children's activities, language skills, social groupings and so forth are seen as significant largely by comparison to those of adults; or are viewed principally as indexes of the particular stages children have reached in the overall progression from childhood to adulthood. Children, as Qvortrup (1994) put it, are seen as becomings rather than beings. The competence paradigm, by contrast, seeks to treat children's actions as significant in their own right; to take children seriously, in analytical terms, as social agents; and to explicate the social competencies which children manifest in the course of their everyday lives as children, with other children and with adults, in peer groups and in families as well as the manifold other arenas of social action.

Among the central questions that have been addressed in this research has been the extent to which children can be said to possess competencies that are somehow unique or specific to the cultures of childhood (Hardman 1973); or alternatively whether the social competence manifested by children is better seen as essentially the same, or of the same order, as that possessed by adults. In either case, explicating the nature and uses of those competencies reveals a picture of childhood as a dynamic arena of social activity involving struggles for power, contested meanings and negotiated relationships, rather than the linear picture of development and maturation made popular by traditional sociology and developmental psychology.

This does not mean denying that children develop; nor that certain aspects of such development can be described in generic rather than idiosyncratic terms. Neither does it mean denying that most forms of 'appropriate' social behaviour are learned rather than being natural. The main thrust of the argument is that the reality of children's social lives cannot be—should not be—reduced to psychological descriptions of the attainment of developmental stages or to sociological accounts of the internalisation of norms. What such reductionism tends to leave out are the practical means by which children put their developing competencies to use in ordinary situations of social conduct; and thus the ways in which children transcend their status as 'developing' or 'learning' through acting, and interacting, as agents rather than objects.[2]

The reductionist picture has infiltrated commonsense in important ways within Western civilisation. Many of Parsons's (1951) ideas about socialisation, like Piaget's (1926) earlier theories of developmental stages in childhood, have become part of ordinary thinking about the role of the family and other institutions in children's social maturation. As Thorne (1993: 13) remarks:

> 'socialisation' and 'development' [are] perspectives that many parents, teachers and other adults *bring* to their interactions with children. As mothers and teachers of young children, women, in particular, are charged with the work of 'developing the child'. But children don't necessarily see themselves 'being socialised' or 'developing' and their interactions with one another, and with adults, extend far beyond these models.... Ask-

---

2. Theories of psychological development that are influenced by Vygotsky (1978) rather than Piaget (1926) have themselves foregrounded this more contextual approach while retaining an emphasis on cognitive development. See for instance Chapman (1988). See also the work of Bruner (1986). These studies take a primarily cognitive and experimental approach, however, and for that reason are not discussed further in the present pages.

ing how children are socialised into adult ways, or how their experiences fit into linear stages of individual development, deflects attention from their present, lived, and collective experiences.

It is precisely this attention to the present, lived and collective experiences of children that the competence paradigm sought to prioritize. In doing so, researchers took account of three main tenets. First, the study of children's social competence should be situated in the empirical circumstances of children's natural, ordinary, everyday lives. Second, those empirical circumstances, or arenas of action, should be seen as both enabling and constraining children's capacities to display social competence. Third, in order to understand the properties of children's situated social competencies, it is necessary to view the relevant social action, as far as possible, endogenously; in other words, to reveal the procedures by which the participants themselves organise and make sense of their activities in a given social context.

A commitment to these three principles raises certain methodological problems. Primarily, how do researchers aiming to meet the third tenet (children's activities should be understood endogenously) actually gain access to the child's perspective? This issue is not confined to research on children and childhood. There is a long-standing tradition in the social sciences of interpretive or phenomenological methodology which has grappled with the problem of how the researcher can come to see the world from the perspective of the researched. The most widespread response in the study of children has been to adopt ethnographic approaches such as participant observation, one-to-one interviews, and the analysis of children's documentary accounts of their lives (James and Prout 1990; Waksler 1991; Thorne 1993; James 1993). James and Prout (1990: 5), for instance, argue that ethnography 'allows children a more direct voice in the production of sociological data than is usually possible through experimental or survey styles of research' (cf. Qvortrup et al., 1994).

Nonetheless, some of the techniques used in ethnographic research are highly problematic when it comes to research on children. For instance, to what extent is it possible for an adult researcher to 'participate' in children's social worlds? Mandell (1991) outlines three types of observer role which progressively move towards a more participatory, or 'least adult', role on the researcher's part. The 'detached observer' role is based on a clear distinction between the social, intellectual and cultural worlds of children and adults, and tends to be the stance adopted by experimental researchers in, for example, developmental psychology. The 'marginal semi-participant' does not go so far as to recognise an absolute distinction but nonetheless believes that the age-based power relation between children and adults can never be transcended. This is a stance typically adopted by researchers using qualitative interviewing techniques. Finally, what Mandell (1991) describes as the 'least-adult' role is based on the idea that 'all aspects of adult superiority except physical differences can be cast aside, allowing the researcher entree into the children's world as an active, fully participating member' (Mandell 1991: 39).

Mandell (1991) herself illustrates some of the difficulties involved in taking up the latter stance; though the kinds of insight it enables may be demonstrated by Goode's (1991) research into the experiential world of deaf-blind children living in a specialist institution. Goode describes how the clinical staff saw the children as virtually feral and hence treated them as almost entirely incompetent. Yet by adopting a form of least-adult role with one child he felt able to begin 'seeing' the world from her perspective. This involved developing a new understanding of her apparently chaotic and self-absorbed behaviour as a competent strategy for managing the contingencies of the institutionalised existence to which she was subjected. The least-adult role in this case involved particularly stringent demands. Goode (1991: 53) refers to one 'thirty-six hour period during which I remained by [Christina's] side'. His aim throughout the research was to use:

> a strategy of 'passive obedience' in which I physically allowed her to take the lead in structuring our interaction. This proved a most beneficial (though difficult to arrive at) stance. Once Chris knew that I was cooperative to this degree, she initiated a huge variety of activities and exchanges *in her terms.*   (Goode 1991: 156, original emphasis)

This suggests that it is possible to gain important insights into the organisation of children's social and experiential worlds by means of a particularised version of participant observation. However, a question that has dogged research based on ethnographic observation in general—not just in relation to childhood—is that of how far the participant observer can be said to arrive at an 'authentic' or 'true' account of the cultures inhabited by other members. This issue may be of particular significance in the case of Goode's (1991) study, because the children whose world he attempted to participate in were deprived of speech and so could not offer any accounts of their own with which Goode might try to validate his observations.[3] Yet even in cases where such members' accounts could be generated, there remains a key problem: that of the essentially indeterminate relationship between the accounts a person might give of his or her behaviours or thoughts ex post facto, and the behaviours or thoughts themselves as they occurred in the original unfolding of interaction. Indeed, it may be difficult to dissociate an account of an action

---

3. A similar problem can be said to be faced by anthropologists attempting ethnographies of cultures whose languages they do not, in the first place, understand. Many classic studies in anthropology contain problems of translation between the cultural practices and symbolic systems of foreign peoples and those with which the (usually White, European or American) anthropologist is familiar. A well-known case is that of Azande witchcraft as described by Evans-Pritchard (1936). This study was at the heart of a later influential debate on the nature of social scientific claims about cultural practices between Winch (1970a, b) and MacIntyre (1970a, b).

from an account *for* an action, in the sense that the researcher has no way of knowing whether the member's after-the-event account is inflected by his or her expectations about what the researcher might be wanting to know.

One attempt to deal with this problem is represented by research in conversation analysis and related approaches which focus attention on the structures and patterns of children's talk, in their peer groups as well as with adults, in natural settings of social interaction. In such research, it is not the case that the researcher makes attempts to enter the social, behavioural or cognitive worlds of children in the ways recommended by advocates of participant observation. Rather, research focuses on the organisation of children's interactions with others in given natural settings as a way of revealing how they themselves make sense—publicly and for each other—of one another's actions in the world.

It is important to look in more detail at this type of research, not only because of the present book's focus on children's talk in counselling, but also in terms of wider methodological debates in childhood studies. In their oft-quoted advocacy of ethnography as the most suitable method for the new social studies of childhood, Prout and James (1990) explicitly contrasted ethnographic observation and interviewing with survey and experimental research, as if these are the only alternatives. Yet other methodologies which focus closely on the organisation of children's verbal and non-verbal interactions, both among themselves and with adults, can reveal a depth and range of interactional competence that for long remained unremarked in the sociology of childhood.

Children's talk and social competence

Children's talk has been studied from a wide range of disciplinary backgrounds, including psychology (developmental, cognitive and social), sociolinguistics, anthropology (cultural, linguistic and social), education, and sociology. Within these disciplines, two types of research can be identified. One type prioritises the development of linguistic skills that children acquire on the way to becoming competent members of the surrounding adult language culture (that is, it takes a developmental perspective). The second type prioritises the linguistic competence that children possess and manifest as part of their membership of the indigenous language cultures of childhood, which can be more or less independent of adults (in other words, it adopts a more competence-based approach). A related distinction can be drawn between research which focuses primarily on children's talk in interaction with adults, and that which addresses the talk of children among their peers.

These strands of interest are not necessarily mutually exclusive. In areas such as the study of children's argument, for example, a concern with how children develop skills in argumentation as they grow older often exists alongside, and in mutual interchange with, concerns with how arguing is an arena of social action in which children manage relationships among peers, with siblings and with adults (for example, Maynard 1985, 1986; Eder 1991; Sheldon 1992a, 1992b, 1996). Here, as in many other areas of childhood studies, traditional disciplinary boundaries (such as that between psychological interests in development and cognition, and sociological interests in institutions and social relationships) begin to blur.

Of key relevance for the present book is work on children's talk using the methods of conversation analysis, where there is now a good deal of research showing how talk and other activities represent resources through which children, as social participants or members of a culture, display interactional competence both in peer groups and among adults. As noted earlier, and expanded in Chapter 2, CA aims to gain access to the ways in which participants make sense of one another's actions and establish collaborative courses of social activity in real time, by studying the sequential relationships between utterances as they occur in the course of talk-in-interaction. This results in a novel take on the importance of ordinary talk, not as a means of obtaining information *about* social organisation and competencies, as in interviews, but as a medium for displaying those things in its own right. CA's focus is on 'how competent members use talk socially to act out the ordinary scenes of their everyday life' (Goodwin 1990: 286). Goodwin (1990: 287) usefully contrasts this approach with conventional ethnographies based on gathering members' accounts of their everyday lives:

> By making use of the techniques of conversation analysis and the documentation of the sequential organisation of indigenous events, we can avoid the pitfalls of 'interpretive anthropology', which tends to focus its attention on ethnographer/informant dialogue rather than interaction *between participants*. This will enable us to move... towards an 'anthropology of experience' concentrating on how people themselves actually perform activities.

CA's interest in children's talk is related to a wider set of interests in sociolinguistics where researchers have sought to determine the specific competencies displayed by children in deploying linguistic resources and managing interaction. Much of this work has been pathbreaking in terms of situating children as competent manipulators of complex verbal and interactional resources (Garvey 1984; Ochs 1988; Ochs and Schieffelin 1979, 1983; Schieffelin 1990). However, much of it is nevertheless couched within an overarching developmental framework in which children are seen as passing through stages marked by factors such as the increasing sophistication of sentence structures and the growing ability to engage in complex interactional structures.

This developmental emphasis has meant that sociolinguistic research has tended to restrict itself to studying children in interaction with adults: in the nursery, the classroom, or with parents. Such an emphasis, as Goodwin (1990) is keen to point out, can result in a downplaying of children's skills in verbal communication among themselves and in their own spaces: even though as Ervin-Tripp and Mitchell-Kernan (1977:7) observed, 'many of the speech events in which children engage typically occur among children apart from adults, and they are explicitly taught, in many cases, by children.'

Goodwin's (1990) work was among the first to provide a full-length study of children's peer group talk using the methods of conversation analysis. She analysed the talk of children in a Black urban neighbourhood of Philadelphia, using the standard CA technique of tape-recording the children's talk in a natural setting: that of play on the streets near their homes. These data enabled her to demonstrate a wide range of ways in which children use language actively to create social organisation among themselves. They include managing the rules and orders of participation in games; collaborating in complex, multi-party tasks; telling stories and other narratives; instigating accusations and constructing defences; and managing arguments in a variety of contexts. In the latter case, one particularly interesting example involves a dispute format used, it seems, largely by girls and called 'he-said-she-said', in which one participant accuses a second of having said something derogatory about her to a third person behind the first's back. Unravelling examples of this interactionally complex form of 'instigating', Goodwin reveals the competent construction of a whole set of situated, contingent social identities among the disputants:

> Within the he-said-she-said confrontation, a field of negotiated action, complete with its own relevant history, is invoked through the structure of an ... accusation ... ; a single utterance creates a complex past history of events, providing operative identity relationships for participants. (Goodwin 1990:286)

Studies such as this, in focusing on children's talk among their peer groups in natural settings of social interaction,

> show how language interaction plays a central role in shaping the social worlds in which children exist to a large extent independently of adults. In these settings, children demonstrate communicative skills which have more to do with being proficient participants within their own culture, than with learning how to become competent members of an adult speech community. (Thornborrow 1998:135)

While work on peer group interaction is significant in revealing more about how talk operates in children's own social worlds, it is nevertheless important to keep in mind the fact that children spend a good deal of their time in adult-controlled institutions: principally school classrooms and the family home (Mayall 1994b; McHoul 1978); though research has also considered interaction between children and medical practitioners (Silverman 1987) and in social service settings such as, in the present case, child counselling. These often involve professionals and other organisational representatives whose task it is to interact with children. One of the key themes to be drawn out in relation to such settings is the way in which differing agendas—and in many ways, differing moral imperatives—can inform the participation of adults and children, and how that can be revealed through a focus on talk.

For example, in a study based on video recording of children in the play section of a kindergarten, Danby and Baker (1998) showed how children, while subject to construction in the terms of institutional knowledge and practices, can deploy their own knowledge of institutional regimes to create spaces of autonomy and resistance. Their data reveal the kindergarten children responding to a teacher's intervention in their conflicts by adopting two parallel strategies. In the teacher's presence, they openly comply with her programmatic attempt to alleviate the conflict and get the children to 'make up'. But once the teacher departs, the children's talk changes as they deploy their own, quite different procedures for dealing with conflict. Teacher-defined knowledge in which conflict is a hurtful thing and in which the hurt one must be comforted by the perpetrator therefore exists in parallel with alternative knowledges which are defined by children themselves and deployed in the interstices of the school's regime.

Similar themes of resistance and alternative practices animate work by Baker (1982, 1984) on adult-adolescent interaction in educational settings, and by Silverman (1987) on interactions between pediatricians and children in clinical settings for conditions such as cleft palate and diabetes. In each of these environments, albeit in very different ways, the interaction is characterised by adult attempts to ensure changes in behaviour by the child, or to manage and regulate children's behaviours according to professionally defined agendas. Perhaps unsurprisingly, children often resist these attempts; however the important thing is to see such resistance, when it occurs, as itself an indication of interactional competence.

Silverman, Baker and Keogh (1998) pursue this point in their study of parent–teacher interviews—a space in which children are present but at the same time the objects of discussion between adults. Focusing on cases of 'silent' children in these contexts, they show how silence (or lack of response from the child) often follows turns in which adults (mainly teachers) have proffered advice for future actions (such as 'maybe you can agree to work harder…'). But the silence is treated in this study not as evidence of deficiency but as a competent strategy by which the child can avoid implication in the moral universe being set up between the parent and teacher. In other words, it is a strategy of resistance in this form of institutional setting:

> Faced with the ambivalence built into such questions and comments by teachers (and parents), silence can be treated as a display of interactional competence. This is because silence (or at least lack of verbal response) allows children to avoid implication in the

collaboratively accomplished adult moral universe and thus . . . enables them to resist the way in which an institutional discourse serves to frame and constrain their social competencies.   (Silverman, Baker and Keogh 1998: 220).

The two themes that animate most of the work discussed in this section—children's competence as conversational participants in their own right, and children's competence in relation to the imperatives and agendas of adult-controlled environments—come together in the child counselling discourse that is the topic of the present book. The rationale underpinning child counselling is that children are given a space to speak in their own terms—without the potential influence of their parents, for example—about their lives, experiences and feelings. Yet seen from a different angle, the child counselling session is an institutional event in which children are subject to the expectation that they *should* speak about such themes; and crucially, the topics that children are encouraged to address may not be topics they want to address. Therefore, the discourse of child counselling occupies its own potentially contradictory space, in which counsellors and children may have differing aims, intentions and agendas. This represents just one of the key themes to be unfolded in the coming chapters.

I mentioned above three tenets of research within the competence paradigm: (1) researchers should focus on the empirical circumstances of children's natural everyday lives; (2) those empirical circumstances should be seen as both enabling and constraining the display of children's social competence; and (3) to understand the properties of those competencies it is necessary to view the relevant social action endogenously (as far as that is possible). We have now reflected on some of the issues involved in tenets (1) and (3). It is important now to say more about what is meant by the second tenet.

Child counselling as an 'arena of action'

If we are to see children as competent social agents, then their competencies should be understood as practical achievements of concrete actors in concrete circumstances. We should not think of social competence in the abstract, as a 'right' accorded to children by adults, which can thus be redefined or taken away by adults. Rather, social competence is something children work at possessing on their own terms, the display of which is an active and agentic achievement. Nevertheless, this achievement is undeniably bounded by the structural features of the milieux in which children live their lives. These 'arenas of action' include the priorities of politics and policy-making: adult-driven attempts to structure the institutionalised worlds of childhood. But they also include the nature of children's relationships with each other and with adults, both inside and outside families and peer groups. In thinking about children and childhood, therefore, it is necessary to link the social competencies integral to children's real-world activities with the structural and interactional frameworks of arenas of action: we need to 'account for children as both constrained by structure and as agents acting in and upon structure' (Prout and James 1990: 28).

This leads us away from one particular conception of children and social competence, which takes what I will describe as an 'incremental' view. Among the common-sense ways of thinking about competence is to see it as the mastery of some task or task-domain. For instance, children may be expected to be competent at dressing themselves at a certain stage in their life; or they may be expected to attain competence at various levels of language use. Such usages, of course, imply a developmental model that sees children mainly as learning to be competent in adult terms. Other senses of 'competence' to be found in the English dictionary include efficiency, capacity and legal power; and this sense of competence as adequate membership, especially in the legal sense, has underpinned both social science research, in some cases, and legislation itself (for instance, the UK Children Act 1989).

The incremental view is in some sense also a moral view: it holds that children should be accorded 'more' social competence, or allowed to possess greater reflexivity about their own circumstances and activities. Thus, some ethnographic research has sought to give children more of an authorial presence in social scientific accounts of their lives (James 1993); survey research has aimed to give children more autonomy by enabling them to act as respondents in their own right instead of relying on the accounts of parents and caregivers (Qvortrup 1990); and legislation has provided new opportunities for children to bring complaints, to initiate legal action in relation to where they live and over issues of parental access, as well as bringing extensions to the requirements to seek children's consent in many circumstances including medical procedures (Archard 1993; Alderson 1993).

A contrasting view—one that I adopt in this book—is that competence should be seen in terms of the situated ability to manage the practical contingencies of social interaction in given contexts. Thus, the question should not be whether children are competent *enough* (from the point of view of adult caregivers, policy makers or social scientists), but what are the practical competencies that children do display in their management of social surroundings? This is to ask how children competently manipulate material and cultural resources at hand in order to engage in contextually appropriate behaviours: behaviours that are appropriate from the perspective of participants themselves, whether other children, adults, or a combination of both.

This leads on to two important points. First, competence is not a unitary phenomenon; and its development is not something that can be traced in any strict linear, stage-type fashion. Rather, the possession or display of competence is something that is established in situ, for any particular here-and-now occasion. This possession and display is something that children themselves may negotiate, argue about and struggle over in local occasions of action, and is certainly not merely a function of the attainment of some specific stage of childhood development.

The second point is that competence is therefore an intrinsically contextual matter: it cannot be separated from the structural contexts in which it is displayed or negotiated. Neither can social competence be understood simply as a property of individuals. Whether it is with other children or with adults, in everyday situations of peer group play or in more formal, adult-framed settings, children's manipulation of culturally available resources is interactionally situated, defined and redefined in the light of others' actions in the setting.[4]

With these remarks in mind, it is possible to see child counselling as an 'arena of action' with particular characteristics. First of all, as said earlier in this chapter, it is an institutional environment intended primarily as a space in which children can speak on their own terms, and in their own words, about their experiences of family break-up. Those adopting an 'incremental' approach might therefore celebrate this as an extension of children's ability to 'be heard' in relation to family circumstances caused by decisions of their parents. But from the alternative, 'situated action' angle, the question is one of *how* children talk in the arena of the child counselling session. What are the resources, cultural, material and interactional, that they marshal in order to manage participation in that setting? And what are the ways in which contextual features of the setting itself—including, perhaps most importantly, the impact of the counsellor's actions in relation to the child—enable and constrain the child's display of social competence?

This relates to a set of issues that will gain in significance as the analysis unfolds in subsequent pages. Child counselling is both an arena of action and a form of institutional discourse. Although I say more about the nature of institutional discourse in Chapter 2, it is important to point out that in general, institutions are things that sociologists 'do not have a very apt way of classifying' (Goffman 1961: 15). For instance, sociologists may talk of the family as a social institution, while at the same time wanting to distinguish the institution of the law court in which formal decisions can be made about how individual families deal with the fact that they are breaking up.

Conversation analysts have developed a particular procedural way of defining 'institutional settings' that usefully distinguishes them—at least for analytical

---

4. As noted earlier (n. 2), this position bears some similarities with the Vygotskian approach within cognitive psychology.

purposes—from other, more 'mundane' settings for social interaction.[5] Forms of institutional discourse are said to be distinguished by two core features: they are 'basically task-related and they involve at least one participant who represents a formal organisation of some kind' (Drew and Heritage 1992: 3). In other words, the participants should be in the setting for some particular reason—to be interviewed for a job, to seek medical advice on an ailment, to participate in the lesson prepared by the teacher, etcetera—and at least one should be a representative of, or responsible to, the organisation for which that interactional task is a relevant or necessary one (a manager, a doctor, a teacher, and so on).

Thus defined, institutions that specifically involve children have traditionally offered little opportunity for children's 'voices' to be heard. This is often reflected in children's own perception of their position in certain institutional environments. In school, for example, Mayall (1994) has shown that children tend to view themselves not as active, autonomous agents but as projects, the objects of the institution's socialisation work. In situations requiring treatment by medical professionals, especially surgery, it has not been the child's view but that of their parents or guardians which governs whether or not treatment will be given (Alderson 1993). A similar circumstance has tended to dominate in the context of legal decisions over matters of residence and contact in cases of parental separation and divorce. As Michels and Prince (1992: 2) put it, 'In the past, attitudes have been paternalistic and intervention has often been with little regard for the child's wishes.'

The various legislative moves mentioned above sought to change this situation by prioritising the view that 'the child is a person, not an object of concern' (Michels and Prince 1992: 2). As applied to situations in which legal and professional representatives face decisions over the welfare of a child (for instance, in relation to medical treatment, child care, child protection, and so forth), the principal ethos here is 'to listen to the child's wishes and feelings, and to treat children with respect as individuals'; hence, 'children of sufficient maturity should be consulted on issues such as placements, reviews and long-term planning' (Michels and Prince 1992: 2).

We can see clearly how this ethos chimes in with the development of social scientific thinking about children and childhood, as outlined earlier. What should also become clear is the way in which child counselling, with its focus on one-to-one dialogue between counsellor and child in the absence of parents, links centrally into the ethos of recent legislation in relation to decisions over family separation. This is what makes the case of child counselling interesting not just in terms of a

---

5. This distinction between 'institutional' and 'mundane' settings is itself somewhat tricky, of course. For one thing, a circuit judge may come to regard the routines and procedures of the courtroom (a canonical 'social institution') as 'mundane' if he or she spends five days a week sitting in judgement on cases.

conversation analytic concern with children's talk in institutional settings; but also in terms of a wider sociological interest in children's social competence and the arenas of action in which that competence is manifested.

Outline of the book

The present chapter has been a general introduction to the sociological context in which the research on which the book is based originally came into existence. I began by outlining the central features of the type of child counselling that the book studies. Then a broader set of issues were discussed including the sociological study of children, with a particular emphasis on their linguistic skills in interaction both among themselves and with adults; and the nature of children's social competence, especially in institutional contexts.

Chapter 2 is an introduction to conversation analysis, the methodological approach adopted in the main part of the book. The first half of the chapter consists of a technical account of the procedures of data collection and analysis undertaken in this approach. The second half describes the approach to so-called institutional discourse that conversation analysts have adopted. Here, I offer an account of child counselling as a particular type of institutional interaction, and the final two sections of this chapter ('CA, social organisation and institutional contexts' and 'Institutional interaction, task-orientation and bricolage') lay some important conceptual groundwork in preparation for what follows.

Chapters 3 to 6 represent the empirical heart of the book. Each of them analyses in detail some aspect of the interaction between counsellors and children. Chapter 3 starts from the position of describing aspects of the data collection method used in the study. However, it quickly moves to a discussion of how the tape recorder that was placed in the counselling room is used as an interactional resource by both counsellors and children. Far from being the methodological concern that it is for some schools of thought in social science, the presence of a tape recorder is shown to be involved in various aspects of the production of counselling talk itself.

Chapter 4 delves deeper into the analysis of 'therapeutic vision', or counsellors' ways of attempting to 'see' therapeutic objects in the often tangential talk of children. Focusing on the use of 'perspective-display' sequences, it reveals how counsellors routinely seek to topicalise certain kinds of perspectives on events while children resist uptake of such topics. In a similar vein, Chapter 5 analyses 'formulations' as another frequently used device for topicalising therapeutic interpretations of children's utterances.

The interface between counsellors' attempts to define therapeutic objects and children's reluctance to engage with such matters is brought into sharp focus in

Chapter 6, which involves a case study of a particularly striking example of child resistance to the counselling agenda. Finally, Chapter 7 draws together some of the implications of the empirical analyses in terms of institutional discourse, the sociological analysis of power in interaction, and the professional concerns of child counselling.

CHAPTER 2

Child counselling as institutional interaction

Before proceeding to empirical case studies, it is necessary to outline the methodological approach taken in the book. As remarked in Chapter 1, that approach is 'conversation analysis' (CA), a method whose name belies the breadth of its application in the study of language and social interaction. Far from being concerned only with everyday conversation, CA's practitioners have analysed a vast range of forms of talk in what are broadly referred to as 'institutional settings' (Drew and Heritage 1992; Arminen 2005). Thus, CA can readily be applied to the analysis of child counselling discourse. In this chapter I begin by describing the basic commitments, research techniques and analytical strategies of CA, before moving to explore how CA can provide an account of child counselling as a form of institutional interaction.

Conversation analysis: Origins and overview

CA emerged in the pioneering research of Harvey Sacks into the structural organisation of everyday language use, at the University of California in the 1960s (see Sacks 1992). Influenced both by ethnomethodological concerns with members' methods of practical reasoning (through his association with Harold Garfinkel [Garfinkel 1967]), and by Erving Goffman's explorations of the structural properties of face-to-face interaction (Goffman 1959, 1961), Sacks initiated a radical research programme designed to investigate the levels of social order which could be revealed in the everyday practice of talking.

The hypothesis with which this programme was begun is that ordinary conversation is not a trivial, random, unorganised phenomenon but a deeply ordered, structurally organised social practice. This hypothesis could best be explored, Sacks reasoned, through the use of naturally-occurring data which could be recorded, transcribed and therefore examined in close detail on repeated occasions. The resulting commitment to tape-recording data rather than relying on ethnographic observation and note-taking was very new at that time. Sociologists and linguists were not generally using recorded materials in the early 1960s, and indeed the only social scientists who were, other than Sacks, were the fairly small group of specialists on body movement, gesture and gaze working with, or influenced by, Birdwhistell (1952) and Bateson (1956; Bateson and Mead 1942) (see McQuown 1971).

Initially, Sacks worked on whatever data he could get hold of. In the earliest days these were recordings of calls to a Los Angeles Suicide Prevention Center. While retaining a sensitivity to the troubles of the persons whose talk he was studying, Sacks began to develop a unique approach to the study of ordinary language, one which focused on the methods by which people manage the routine exchange of turns at talk while minimising gap and overlap between them, and on the sequential patterns and structures associated with the management of social activities in conversation.

As these investigations progressed, and through his collaboration with colleagues including Emanuel Schegloff and Gail Jefferson, the available data were supplemented with expanding corpora of more 'mundane' telephone calls; and subsequently expanded beyond the domain of telephone interactions to study video recordings of interactions with the aim of analysing the integration of speech with non-vocal activities. CA has also been used within a broader framework to analyse the distinctive methods of turn-taking and activity organisation found in specialised settings such as courts of law (Atkinson and Drew 1979), classrooms (Mehan 1979), broadcast news interviews (Greatbatch 1988), public speeches (Atkinson 1984) and many others (Drew and Heritage 1992).

In all these applications, CA's aim is to reveal how the technical aspects of speech exchange represent structured, socially organised resources by which participants perform and co-ordinate activities through talk-in-interaction. Talk is treated as a vehicle for social action; and also as the principal means by which social organisation in person-to-person interaction is mutually constructed and sustained. Hence it is a strategic site in which social agents' orientation to and evocation of the social contexts of their interaction can be empirically investigated. Later in this chapter, I discuss in more detail the nature of these investigations into 'institutional' forms of talk and their significance for the analysis of child counselling discourse.

What counts as data: Tapes and transcripts

Conversation analysis focuses its attention on recordings of 'naturally occurring' spates of talk-in-interaction.[1] These are transcribed using a system which is intended to capture in fine detail the characteristics of the sequencing of turns, including gaps, pauses and overlaps; and elements of speech delivery such as audible breath and laughter, stress, enunciation, intonation and pitch.[2]

---

[1]. An interesting debate on the notion of 'naturally-occurring' data can be found in the papers by Speer (2003a, b), Lynch (2003), Potter (2003) and ten Have (2003).

[2]. A full account of CA's transcription procedures can be found in Chapter 3 of Hutchby and Wooffitt (1998).

Initially, CA researchers restricted their attention mainly to recordings of telephone conversations (Hopper 1992). Since then, video-recordings have become more widely used. However, CA's explicit focus on the organisation of talk-in-interaction means that gesture, body movement and facial expression tend not to be studied in their own right, as may be the case in the field of interactional kinesics (Kendon 1990), but rather in exploring the relationships *between* speech and body movement. It is entirely feasible, within CA, to analyse audio-only recordings even when the participants have visual access to one another. For instance, Goodwin (1990), in a detailed study of the management of disputes among children at play on the street, was able to develop a compelling analysis of the role of talk in the social organisation of the children's groups using as her data only an audio record supplemented by ethnographic fieldnotes.

It is important to stress that, for CA, it is the tape-recording rather than the transcript which is thought of as the primary data. The aim is to analyse the data (the recorded interaction) using the transcript as a convenient referential tool. The transcript is thus seen as a 'representation' of the data; while the tape recording is viewed as a 'reproduction' of a determinate social event. Of course, the tape is only one form of reproduction; and whether it is an audiotape or a videotape, it does not reproduce everything that went on in the vicinity of the recording device during the time it was switched on. At the same time, clearly there are innumerable phenomena in any given stretch of talk which could be transcribed to varying levels of detail. No transcription system exists which is able, or lays claim to being able, to capture all the possible features of talk that may be observable. As Kendon (1982: 478) remarked:

> It is a mistake to think that there can be a truly neutral transcription system, which, if only we had it, we could then use to produce transcriptions suitable for any kind of investigation... Transcriptions, thus, embody hypotheses.

Similarly, Ochs (1979: 44) describes transcription as 'a selective process reflecting theoretical goals and definitions'. This is no less true of CA transcription. A CA transcript embodies in its format and in the phenomena it marks out the analytic concerns which conversation analysts bring to the data. These concerns are of two types. First, the dynamics of turn-taking. On this level, transcripts seek to capture the details of the beginnings and endings of turns taken in talk-in-interaction, including precise details of overlap, gaps and pauses, and audible breathing. Second, the characteristics of speech delivery. Here, transcripts mark noticeable features of stress, enunciation, intonation and pitch.

In the following sections I will illustrate some of the technical aspects of how conversation analysts go about analysing talk-in-interaction. These aspects will be discussed using one extract from a transcription of ordinary conversation. My reasons for beginning with such a piece of data in preference to an excerpt from a child counselling session are twofold. First, I wish to point out a wide range of generic features of conversational turn-taking in the most economical way, and the particular extract I will use enables this. Second, my analysis of child counselling talk in subsequent chapters relies at least partly on the idea that child counselling represents a specialised form of turn-taking in relation to everyday conversation. It is therefore important to begin by providing the baseline in terms of which that very specialisation can be appreciated. It is one of the core claims of CA that the speech exchange system of ordinary or 'casual' conversation provides speakers with the greatest range of free variability in key matters of turn length, turn order and turn content; whereas forms of 'institutional' discourse (such as child counselling) are characterised by varying degrees of restriction in terms of those three parameters. This is an issue that I return to discuss at greater length later in the present chapter, when the significance of CA to the analysis of child counselling in particular is explained.

Turn-taking: Some basic observations

Following is an initially unremarkable extract of conversation recorded during a telephone call.[3] However, as we look in detail at the transcript, it reveals a wide range of the most basic aspects of the organisation of talk-in-interaction that have been described within conversation analysis. We start, in line 1, at the beginning of the conversation, just as Nancy picks up the phone to answer Edna's call. The full set of transcription conventions used here is provided in the Glossary.

(1) NB:II:2: 1–2

```
1    Nancy:   Hello:,
2    Edna:    .hh HI::.
3             (.)
4    Nancy:   Oh: 'i:::='ow a:re you Edna:,
5    Edna:    FI:NE yer LINE'S BEEN BUSY.
6    Nancy:   Yea:h (.) my u-fuhh! h- .hhhh my fa:ther's wife
7             ca:lled me,h .hhh So when she ca:lls me::, h I
8             always talk fer a lo:ng ti:me cuz she c'n afford it
9             en I ca:n't.hhh [hhhh [huh]
10   Edna:                    [↑OH:[:::  ]: my [go:sh=Ah ↑th]aht=
```

---

3. Many of the data extracts presented in this chapter come from the author's personal library of tapes and transcripts of conversation, most of them originally made (and transcribed) by other researchers in conversation analysis.

Chapter 2. Child counselling as institutional interaction 23

```
11   Nancy:                          [↑↑AOO:::::hh!]
12   Edna:    =my phone wuz outta order:
13            (0.2)
14   Nancy:   n[:No::?
15   Edna:    [I called my sister en I get this busy en then I'd
16            hang up en I'd lift it up again id be: busy.
17            (0.9)
18   Edna:    .hh How you doin'.
19   Nancy:   .t hhh Pretty good I gutta rai:se.h .hh[hh
20   Edna:                                          [Goo:u[d.
21   Nancy:                                               [Yeh
22            two dollars a week.h
23            (.)
24   Edna:    Oh [wo:w.
25   Nancy:      [↑Ih:::huh hu[:h huh,
26   Edna:                    [Wudee gun: do with it a:ll.
27   Nancy:   Gol' I rilly I jis' don't know how Ah'm gunnuh
28            spend all that money.
29            (0.2)
30   Edna:    Y'oughta go sho:pping.
31   Nancy:   .hhhh Well I should but (.) yihknow et eight
32            dollars a mo:[n:th:,   anything   I'd] buy'd, be using=
33   Edna:                 [hm hmm hm-mm-hm. ]
34   Nancy:   =up my raise fer 'alf [a YEA:R:] ((smile voice))
35   Edna:                          [Ye:a:h. ]
36   Edna:    .hhhhh Bud j's lef' t' play go:lf he's gotta go tuh
37            Riverside...
```

This transcript shows a number of relevant features of the socially organised nature of talk-in-interaction. At the most basic level, it is designed to display how the talk is organised into a series of turns. For conversation analysis, however, turns do not just occur in a serial order (one turn followed by another, and so on): they are sequentially organised (Sacks 1987). That is to say, there are orderly ways in which one turn is related to a next; and in which turns are therefore coordinated into patterned sequences through which particular activities are accomplished. That orderliness is described by treating the transitions between turns as revealing two kinds of things. First, 'next turn' is the place in which speakers display their understanding of a prior turn's possible completion. Second, next turns are places where speakers display their understanding of a prior turn's 'content,' or more specifically, the action it has been designed to do.

In terms of the first issue, we find that overwhelmingly, turn-transitions are coordinated by participants with minimal gap and overlap between utterances. Note in the transcript above, for instance, that only five between-turn gaps occur (in lines 3, 13, 17, 23 and 29), and the longest of these is no more than two-tenths of a second. (I return to the issue of overlaps presently.) Participants are able to achieve this level of coordination between turn endings and next turn beginnings because of a basic set of features in the actual make-up of turns themselves.

Sacks, Schegloff and Jefferson (1974) proposed that turns are made up of 'turn-constructional units' (TCUs)—examples are: a sentence, a clause, a phrase, or a single word such as 'Hello'—which are recognisable by members of a language culture. The end of any TCU represents a point at which a next speaker may legitimately make a bid for the floor. Sacks et al. captured this feature by referring to TCUs as presenting 'transition-relevance places' (TRPs) at their completion. At a TRP, a candidate next speaker may, but need not, attempt to take a turn; while a current speaker may, but need not, attempt to produce a next TCU. Current speakers may also select a next speaker, in which case the one selected is obliged to take a turn at that point. These rules for turn-taking are context-free: that is, they allow for such local contextual variations as the identities and number of speakers, length and content of turns, and so on. But they are also context-sensitive in that they apply to the local circumstances of particular turns in particular conversations.

The crucial point about these rules is that they are observably oriented to by members. An orientation to the possible completion of a turn at TCU completion, and the legitimate relevance of turn-transition at that point, can be illustrated using the extract above if we focus on the occurrence of overlap. On the face of it, overlapping talk may be considered evidence of an incoming speaker's failure adequately to attend to the status of a current speaker's turn: that is, they might be seen as starting 'too early' on their turn; or starting up at a point where the turn has not yet reached a recognisable transition-relevance place. However, it is possible to show that most instances of overlap in extract 1 (marked with left brackets, [, for onset and right brackets,], for cessation) clearly occur in the environment of TRPs (see Jefferson 1986).

For instance, in line 9, what Edna's 'OH:::::' overlaps is a quiet laugh particle, 'hhh hhh huh,' which Nancy fits onto the end of a TCU: 'So when she calls me::, h I always talk fer a lo:ng ti:me cuz she c'n afford it en I ca:n't.' In line 21, what Nancy overlaps is the last phoneme of a recognisable TCU: Edna's assessment, 'Goo:ud,' of Nancy's announcement 'I gutta rai:se.'

Other instances appear more complex, but can still be accounted for as orderly. For instance at line 11, Nancy's 'AOO:::::hh!' is a high-pitched laugh, which seems to be produced in overlap with—but prior to the recognisable completion of—Edna's remark that she thought her phone was out of order (since she had tried numerous times to get through). However, notice that in her immediately prior turn Nancy had offered a joke of sorts about talking on the phone for a long time when her father's wife calls, 'cuz she c'n afford it en I ca:n't.' She then begins quietly to laugh. Edna's turn is begun with a loud, and high-pitched 'OH::::: my go:sh,' to which Nancy responds with her similarly-pitched 'AOO:::::hh!' Possibly, then, Nancy hears the action that Edna is doing as that of responding to her joke, and starts to laugh by reference to 'OH::::: my go:sh' as a recognisable, and possibly complete, joke-response. The overlap is complicated because Edna carries on her turn, following up Nancy's quip by herself quipping about the length of time Nancy's phone has been engaged: 'OH::::: my go:sh=Ah thaht my phone wuz outta order.'

Focusing on this instance of overlap, and wondering why it occurs in the places that it does, illustrates a principal policy of conversation analysis, and also suggests the analytical pay-off from that policy. The policy is to treat anything that occurs in talk-in-interaction as possibly orderly—to dismiss no detail a priori as disorderly, trivial, or irrelevant. The pay-off is that we thereby gain an insight into the nature of participants' own understandings of what is going on at any moment in interaction, as displayed in the ways their turns address the turns they are sequentially next to.

Exhibiting understanding in the next turn

CA's interest in how the sequential organisation of talk can be used to reveal the ways participants exhibit understanding of one another's utterances can be illustrated further with the use of data from the second half of Extract (1). In line 19, Nancy announces that she 'gutta rai:se.' By the end of the extract, it is evident that the raise has been presented as, and understood to be, a 'lousy' raise: Nancy is dissatisfied with it; indeed it was hardly worth getting. However, none of these things are said outright. The presentation of the raise as a lousy raise is achieved entirely indirectly. A central resource used by Nancy here is that of irony. What is interesting to note is the way that ironical complaint, and its uptake, emerge in the course of a sequence of talk in which Edna's understanding of Nancy's meaning is observably modified.

The sequence begins at line 18, when Edna inquires, 'How you doin'.' This inquiry reciprocates Nancy's earlier ''ow a:re you Edna:' (line 4); the intervening 13 lines having been taken up with the talk occasioned by Edna's remark 'yer LINE'S BEEN BUSY'.

In line 21, Nancy's response to Edna's inquiry begins: 'Pretty good.' A first thing to note is that 'Pretty good' is a different kind of response to a 'How are you' inquiry to the response that Edna had given earlier—i.e., 'FI:NE.' 'Fine' represents the conventional response to 'How are you' (Sacks 1975); it is a no-problem response.

'Pretty good,' on the other hand, represents what Jefferson (1980) describes as a 'downgraded conventional response'. Although it appears very similar to 'Fine,' one kind of work which 'Pretty good' can do that 'Fine' does not is to adumbrate bad news. Basically, if a speaker has some bad news to report or some trouble to tell, one way of managing that is to use 'Pretty good' in this sequential environment in order to set up a trajectory in which the trouble might be elaborated on. By contrast, use of 'Fine' in this position, although it may be followed by news of some sort, does not seem to be followed by the production of bad news.

Adumbrating bad news, then, is a potential property of a 'Pretty good' response to 'How are you': potential in that bad news may or may not follow, and may or may not be told. This potentiality makes it a perfect kind of resource for Nancy to engage in complaining about her raise ironically, and hence indirectly. The first mention of the raise immediately follows the 'Pretty good' response; and itself takes the form of a straightforward, unelaborated announcement: 'I gutta rai:se.' At this stage, then, the news that is being offered is, it appears, good news. And Edna indeed understands that to be the case, as exhibited in her response in line 20: 'Goo:ud.'

It is only in the next two turns (lines 21–4) that the sense of Nancy's news being not so good in fact emerges. But notice that there is nothing in Nancy's next turn itself—'Yeh two dollars a week.'—which overtly suggests that Edna may need to revise her initial understanding of the news. She does not correct Edna's congratulatory reaction, for instance by saying, 'It's not that good—it's only two dollars a week.' Rather, her turn begins with an affirmation, 'Yeh,' and then goes on simply to name the amount. In other words, the turn does the work of ironicising the news implicitly: it is left up to Edna to recognise the significance of 'two dollars a week,' and so to detect the irony in Nancy's talk.

Edna's reinterpretation of the announcement appears in the next turn, line 24. Notice that while her initial reaction was fitted to the form of the announcement as good news, this second reaction, a downward-intoned 'Oh wo:w.' (the full-stop marking the downward inflection), is equally fitted to the revised status of the news following Nancy's naming of the tiny sum involved. The fact that the turn begins with 'Oh' is also significant here. The discourse marker 'Oh' routinely performs the interactional work of displaying that its producer has undergone some change of state in his or her knowledge (Heritage 1984). Thus, Edna's use of the item here connects with the way she is exhibiting a new understanding of her coparticipant's talk. More importantly, the particular kind of new understanding being exhibited is marked in the enunciation of the 'wo:w' itself. The downward inflection on 'wo:w' marks the bad news—or perhaps more accurately, 'no news'—status to be accorded the raise, just as an alternative, upward and animated inflection ('Oh ↑wow!') would mark the news as something quite different.

Following that, and Nancy's burst of laughter in line 25, Edna works to sustain the joke about the paltriness of the raise by asking, ironically, 'Wudee gun: d̲o with it a:ll' (line 26) and suggesting that Nancy 'oughta go sho̲:pping' (line 30). Nancy's responses to these turns—especially the heavily ironic 'Go̲l- I ri̲lly I ji̲s' don't know how Ah'm gunnuh spe̲nd all tha̲t money' (lines 27–8), in sustaining the irony, work to display to Edna that her revised understanding in fact is the correct one.

These brief remarks on the interactional accomplishment of irony illustrate how the next turn in a sequence can be treated as a systematic locus in which participants in talk-in-interaction establish and maintain a shared orientation on salient aspects of social reality. Furthermore, focusing on the sequential emergence of irony in this instance allows another central issue in CA to be illustrated: that of the relationship between particular social actions and the sequential resources by which they are accomplished. These brief observations on the ironical form and ironical uptake of Nancy's complaint show how indirect actions such as ironical reference are not simply properties of individual speech acts, but are situated features of interaction, achieved in local space and real time.

Adjacency pairs: The conditional relevance of next position

The 'next turn' can also be a place in which more specific interactional constraints are operative. Certain categories of utterance make relevant a circumscribed class of responses in next position. Easily recognisable examples are: a question, which makes an answer relevant as the next move; a greeting, which makes a return greeting relevant in next turn; an invitation, which makes an acceptance or declination relevant in next position; or an accusation, which makes a rebuttal or justification relevant next. These are all representative of adjacency pairs, one of the central concepts in CA research.

The adjacency pair concept illustrates the way in which particular types of utterance can be made conditionally relevant by prior turns. The production of a first part of a pair-type, such as a question, sets up the constraint that a next speaker should respond by producing the relevant second part from that type—in this case, an answer. Moreover, whatever does follow a first pair-part will be monitored for exactly how it works as a response to that move. In other words, not producing something hearable as an answer in the next turn following a question is an accountable event: something for which a participant may be sanctioned, as in the following extract:

(2) TW:M:38
```
1    Child:    Have to cut these Mummy.
2              (1.3)
3    Child:    Won't we Mummy.
4              (1.5)
5    Child:    Won't we.
6    Mother:   Yes.
```

The child first announces that they will 'Have to cut these', then, following a pause (line 2) displays that she was expecting a response of some sort from the mother: in line 3 the child asks her to confirm the initial observation. Getting no response again in the 1.5-second pause in line 4, child pursues that response in line 5, after which the mother finally answers.

By saying that a second pair-part is conditionally relevant given a first, conversation analysts are pointing to something specific about the adjacency pair relationship. It is not that they are merely describing the fact that certain types of turns follow other types (which would be somewhat commonsensical). Rather, they are pointing to the fact that the relationship between adjacency pair-parts is a normative one: in other words, one that has moral dimensions. This can be seen on two levels. First, motivational inferences can be drawn from the non-occurrence of a second part following the production of a first. For instance, not returning a greeting may be taken as a sign of rudeness; not providing an answer to a question may be taken as indicative of evasiveness; while not proffering a defence to an accusation may be taken as a tacit admission of guilt. Second, the oriented-to relevance of second parts following the production of a first can remain in play across time: it is not limited to cases of literal adjacency.

Thus, instances in which, say, a question is followed by another question, rather than an answer, may seem to militate against the force of the adjacency pair concept. But such cases in fact can quite strongly display the temporally extendible relevance of the adjacency pair framework, once we see that the second question routinely represents a first move in an insertion sequence (Levinson 1983: 304–6). Insertion sequences defer a second pair-part's production, but they do not negate its relevance. A speaker may respond to a question such as, 'Can I borrow the car?' with another question: 'How long do you need it?' The response to that inserted question—say, 'Only a couple of hours'—provides a next slot in which a response to the first question is once more relevant and to be monitored for.

Another aspect of the normative properties of adjacency pairs lies in the systematically different ways that recipients of first parts design the alternative actions to be done in second position. Invitations, for instance, can be accepted or declined; requests can be granted or rejected. The significant point is that these alternatives are non-equivalent. That non-equivalence is traced in the features of turn design through which alternative second parts are proffered. Broadly, responses which agree or are congruent with the expectation projected by a first pair-part are produced contiguously and without mitigation. Responses which diverge from that expectation—which in some way disagree—tend to be prefaced by hesitations, discourse markers such as "Well...," and, unlike congruent responses, are accompanied by accounts for why the speaker is responding in this way (Pomerantz 1984; Sacks 1987).

Extracts (3) and (4) show the first type of response, where the second speaker agrees with the assessment produced in the first turn, and their turns are produced immediately and straightforwardly:

(3) JS:II:28
1 Jo: It's a beautiful day out isn't it?
2 Lee: Yeh it's just gorgeous.

(4) VIYMC:1:2
1 Pat: It's a really clear lake isn't it?
2 Les: It's wonderful.

Extract (5), on the other hand, shows someone seeking to decline an invitation, in which rather than straightforwardly and immediately declining, the second speaker produces talk that softens or mitigates the declination. This consists of (a) delaying the start of the turn with a slight laugh ('hehh') and the word 'Well'; (b) issuing an appreciation of the invitation ('that's awfully sweet of you'); and (c) providing an account for why the invitation is being declined:

(5) SBL
1 Mary: Uh if you'd care to come over and visit a little
2   while this morning I'll give you a cup of coffee.
3 Ida: hehh Well that's awfully sweet of you, I don't
4   think I can make it this morning .hh uhm I'm
5   running an ad in the paper and- and uh I have to
6   stay near the phone.

These different response types are termed preferred and dispreferred respectively. The concept of preference in CA is not used to refer to the psychological dispositions or motives of individuals; but to point to just this structural feature of the sequential organisation of some types of adjacency pair. Research has additionally shown that the design features of dispreferred responses can be used as a resource for the maintenance of social solidarity in talk-in-interaction. This is so not only in the way that dispreferred responses may be accompanied by accounts or explanations; but also in the way that hesitations and other means of marking a dispreferred response can provide a source for a first speaker to revise the original first pair-part in such a way as to try and avoid disagreement or rejection (Davidson 1984). This happens in the following extract, where Edna, judging that Nancy may be about to turn down her invitation to come over for lunch, issues a candidate reason for Nancy to decline the invitation (line 4):

(6) NB:II:2: 4
```
1      Edna:    Wanna come down an' have a bite a' lunch with
2               me:?=I got some bee:r en stu:ff,
3               (0.2)
3      Nancy:   Well yer real sweet hon:, uh::m (.) [let- I hav-
4→     Edna:                                       [Or do yuh have
5               sum'pn el[se t-
6      Nancy:            [No: I have to uh call Bob's mother. .h I
7               told 'er I:'d ca:ll 'er this morning.
```

These points bring out again the centrality, for CA, of the inferential properties associated with speakers' moves in interaction sequences. They also address the ways that those inferences have a distinctly moral, or evaluative, dimension. Speakers can be seen not only to be establishing and maintaining mutual understanding of one another's actions in sequences of talk, but also to be holding each other accountable for those actions. In this sense the adjacency pair framework, and the preference organisation that operates for some types of adjacency pair, constitute an important site in which to observe the relationships between patterns of language use and structures of social action.

CA, social organisation and insitutional contexts

Having filled in some detail about the basic concepts and analytical procedures used in CA, we can now begin tying back the points made above to the question of child counselling as a form of talk-in-interaction. In order to do so we have to understand the way that conversation analysts have applied their concerns with turn-taking and its structural phenomena (adjacency pairs, overlap, repair and so on) to other, non-conversational, forms of talk.

The first point to make is that CA seeks to treat talk in and of itself as an organised form of social action. It therefore begins from a broadly structuralist sociological standpoint, as exemplified in the following quotation:

> The initial and most fundamental assumption of conversation analysis is that all aspects of social action and interaction can be examined in terms of conventionalised or institutionalised structural organisations which analysably inform their production. These

> organisations are to be treated as structures in their own right which, like other social institutions or conventions, stand independently of the psychological or other characteristics of particular participants.   (Heritage 1989: 22)

CA approaches recordings of naturally occurring talk with the aim of (a) describing the structural organisations informing its production, and (b) thereby explicating the methods used by participants to engage in mutually intelligible, ordered courses of social interaction.

As the second of these two aims suggests, CA's structuralism is tempered by an action orientation in which members of society are seen as knowledgeable agents actively involved in the intersubjective construction and maintenance of their shared social worlds (in this, it follows the ethnomethodological line established by Garfinkel 1967). The analytical connection between the description of orderly features of talk and the explication of participants' methods of sense-making is neatly formulated in this early statement of methodological policy:

> We have proceeded under the assumption (an assumption borne out by our research) that insofar as the materials we worked with exhibited orderliness, they did so not only for us, indeed not in the first place for us, but for the coparticipants who had produced them. If the materials (records of naturally occurring conversations) were orderly, they were so because they had been methodically produced by members of the society for one another, and it was a feature of the conversations that we treated as data that they were produced so as to allow the display by the coparticipants to each other of their orderliness, and to allow the participants to display to each other their analysis, appreciation and use of that orderliness.   (Schegloff and Sacks 1973: 290)

CA's complementary emphases on the internal structure or design of turns at talk and the organisation of sequences are thus treated as revealing elemental features of social agents' intersubjective 'definitions of the situation' and the procedural means by which they coordinate activities within, and as part of, those situations.

This approach leads to a particularly dynamic view of context which works on a number of interrelated levels. In the first place, CA emphasises the fact that for their producers, utterances do not occur as isolated actions but precisely as actions situated in an ongoing context of social interaction. Such actions, moreover, are always doubly contextualised in the sense that they are both context-shaped and context-renewing:

> Actions are context-shaped in that they are understood, and produced to be understood, in relation to the context of prior utterances and understandings in which they are embedded and to which they contribute. They are context-renewing because every current action forms the immediate context for a next action and will thus tend to renew (i.e. maintain, alter or adjust) any more generally prevailing sense of context which is the object of the participants' orientations and actions.   (Heritage and Greatbatch 1991: 95)

Thus, context is treated as 'both the project and the product of the participants' own actions' (Drew and Heritage 1992: 19). This local production of contexts for action is treated as analysable through investigating the ways that participants, in their means of organising their talk, display for one another (and hence for the analyst too) their understanding and sense of 'what is going on' at any given moment in interaction.

This concern with context as an active accomplishment underpins research into the relationship between talk and wider social contexts, or what are often described as 'institutional settings'. Conversation analysts have examined talk in such settings as courts of law (Atkinson and Drew 1979), classrooms (McHoul 1978), medical consultations (Heath 1992), television and radio studios (Heritage 1985; Clayman and Heritage 2004; Clayman 1988, 1992; Hutchby 1996, 2006), counselling rooms (including, for our purposes, child counselling rooms) (Peräkylä 1995; Silverman 1996) and numerous others (Drew and Heritage 1992; Arminen 2005).

In this work, CA's view of the relevance of context is commensurate with the statements of methodological policy quoted above. That is, at the same time as acknowledging that institutional settings clearly involve participants adopting particular roles and engaging in relatively specialised speaking practices, CA emphasises the active work of participants in rendering these roles and speaking practices into a lived reality. In other words, the observably specialised nature of institutional discourse must be seen as actively produced by participants. Therefore:

> Analysts who wish to depict the distinctively 'institutional' character of some stretch of talk... must... demonstrate that the participants constructed their conduct over its course—turn by responsive turn—so as to progressively constitute and hence jointly and collaboratively realise the occasion of their talk, together with their own social roles in it, as having some distinctively institutional character. (Heritage and Greatbatch 1991:95)

The upshot is that emphasis is placed not on how the setting independently determines the activities, strategies and procedures adopted within it, but on how those activities, strategies and procedures make available (for participants and analysts alike) participants' orientation to, and reproduction of, specialised institutional features of the setting.

This approach is based on a comparative procedure in which the turn-taking system for conversation is used as a benchmark against which other forms of talk-in-interaction may be recognised for their distinctiveness. Ordinary face-to-face conversation is treated, for analytic purposes, as an interactional baseline. In comparative terms, all forms of institutional interaction can be characterised by a systematic reduction and/or specialisation of the array of practices observable in ordinary conversation. This comparative procedure is methodologically powerful in terms of CA's approach to context precisely because it reveals participants' active orientation to differing contexts through a focus on the distinctive details of interaction in different types of environment.

Using this approach, conversation analysts have distinguished two basic types of institutional discourse, referred to by Heritage and Greatbatch (1991) as formal and non-formal. The formal types are represented by courts of law, many kinds of interview—particularly the broadcast news interview—certain kinds of classroom environment, and various ceremonial occasions. In such settings there is a close relationship between the social identities adopted by participants and the types of turn that they produce in interaction. As Heritage and Greatbatch (1991:95) put it, 'the institutional character of the interaction is embodied first and foremost in its form—most notably in turn-taking systems which depart substantially from the way in which turn-taking is managed in conversation'. In activities such as courtroom cross-examination (Atkinson and Drew 1979) or broadcast news interviewing (Greatbatch 1988), speakers adopting particular institutional roles (counsel/witness, interviewer/interviewee) orient to normative restrictions on the production of specific speech activities. Typically, interactions are conducted by means of question-answer sequences in which it is the institutional representative or professional incumbent (i.e. counsel/interviewer) who produces the questions, while the other (witness/interviewee) is restricted to that of answering those questions. Turns which depart from these norms have to be accounted for: that is, speakers in such circumstances may produce turn-components which justify the departure; or in the absence of justifications, their deviation from the norm may be held to account by others in the setting. Turn-taking procedures in formal types of institutional interaction are thus characterised by restricted variability in turn-types and turn-order; whereas in ordinary conversation both turn-type and turn-order are freely variable (Sacks et al., 1974).[4]

However, the category of formal institutional interaction incorporates only a small number of institutional settings: mainly the court in session, various forms of interview, and some of the more 'traditional' pedagogic environments. Far more widespread are what Heritage and Greatbatch (1991:97) refer to as 'non-formal' types, 'commonly occurring in medical, psychiatric, social service, business and related environments'. In such settings, much less uniformity in the patterning of conduct is evident. The interaction may be more or less explicitly directed towards carrying out official tasks such as diagnosing illness (Heath 1992) or making

---

4. Atkinson and Drew (1979), and following them, Drew and Heritage (1992) referred to this using the term 'turn-type pre-allocation'. I prefer to avoid this phrase because, while these authors were clearly adopting the conversation analytic framework and thus referring to orientations by participants and not extraneous constraints imposed by the setting, the word 'pre-allocation' is nevertheless open to interpretation in terms of what Coulter (1982) describes as a 'container' model of institutional context. That is, it can be taken to imply the view that the setting itself 'allocates' turns to participants, rather than participants themselves orienting to what I prefer to describe as the restricted variability of turn-types.

decisions about clients' health or welfare needs (Heritage and Sefi 1992; Bergmann 1992). As a result there may emerge 'aggregative asymmetries in the patterning of activities between role incumbents (e.g., as between doctors and patients in the asking and answering of questions in private consultations)' (Heritage and Greatbatch 1991: 97). But typically these official tasks and activities are managed within turn-taking frameworks that allow for considerable variation, improvisation and negotiation in terms of the participation status or 'footing' (Goffman 1981) adopted by lay and professional participants alike.

For this reason, Heritage and Greatbatch (1991: 98) referred to non-formal types of institutional interaction as having a 'quasi-conversational' character. As they say: 'When considered in turn-taking terms, at least, the boundaries between [non-formal] forms of institutional talk and ordinary conversation can appear permeable and uncertain.'

It is important to acknowledge what is not being claimed here. The term 'quasi-conversational' does not mean that there are no significant differences between turn-taking procedures in non-formal institutional interaction and in conversation. Rather, the 'permeability' and 'uncertainty' of the boundaries between these two general frameworks makes those boundaries often very difficult to identify in principled analytical terms. The 'aggregative asymmetries' referred to above are not provided for on the basis of normative constraints on participation opportunities for speakers in given institutional roles, but rather seem to emerge out of a largely tacit orientation to specific activities associated with the situation's task-oriented work.

Institutional interaction, task-orientation and *bricolage*

The child counselling sessions in my data fall under this latter heading of non-formal institutional interaction. There are no organisational conventions which state, for instance, that counsellors should ask questions and children provide answers. Indeed, textbooks on child counselling practice frequently say just the opposite: 'There is a danger in asking too many questions, because the child may fear being asked to disclose information which is private and/or too scary to share' (Geldard and Geldard 1998: 11). Yet in examining the data, it is evident not only that questions are frequently asked, but that they are far more frequently asked by counsellors than by children. Moreover, the types of questions, statements and other turns taken by counsellors reveal an orientation to the particular task of eliciting talk about feelings, concerns and reasons. This relates to a further set of features in the definition of non-formal institutional interaction. As Drew and Heritage (1992: 28) put it:

systematic aspects of the organisation of sequences (and of turn-design within sequences) having to do with such matters as the opening and closing of encounters, with the ways in which information is requested, delivered and received, with the design of referring expressions, etc., are now beginning to emerge as facets of the way in which the 'institutionality' of such encounters is managed.   (Drew and Heritage 1992: 28)

In his work on AIDS counselling as institutional discourse, Peräkylä (1995) suggested that a term which captures this ad hoc moulding of resources to hand in order to shape the interaction in light of institutional concerns is *bricolage*. *Bricolage* derives from the French verb *bricoler,* meaning 'to tinker', and a *bricoleur* is someone who is adept at utilising materials in ways that they were not originally intended in order to create something new. For that reason it is often associated with the postmodernist movement in art and architecture, and with the fashions of popular and youth subculture, within cultural studies. But for the purposes of this book, I use the term in relation to the features of discourse in non-formal institutional settings. Although few other CA researchers so far have adopted the term,[5] bricolage can readily be applied to many cases of published research showing how observable asymmetries and patterns of turn-taking emerge in the absence of normative constraints on turn-types.

Studies which show these features while not using the term bricolage include Frankel's (1984, 1990) and Heath's (1992) analyses of consultations between physicians and their patients. Frankel noted that while there is no institutionalised rule that constrains patients from producing topically disjunctive questioning turns, overwhelmingly it is the case that topics and questions are initiated by physicians and not by patients. His analysis showed that this asymmetry emerges as a result of a tacitly negotiated state of affairs within the consultation by which, first, physicians typically open up restricted participation opportunities for patients by asking particular kinds of information-seeking questions. Such information-seeking questions make relevant in the next turn (the patient's turn) answers which provide the information sought by the question. Second, Frankel found that patients themselves orient to and reproduce an asymmetrical distribution of participation rights by seeking to introduce new topics of their own largely in the form of turn components tagged onto their responses to physicians' questions. In other words, patient-initiated topics come in the context of physician-initiated questions, thereby 'ensur(ing) that additional information, if it is going to be dealt with, will be handled via a physician-initiated obligation package, i.e., question-answer sequence' (Frankel 1984: 164).

---

5. 'Bricolage' as a central procedure in the management of talk-in-interaction has been foregrounded, though not from a CA perspective, by Erickson (2004).

In a similar vein, Heath (1992) showed how in the course of general practitioner consultations, patients tacitly orient to and reproduce an asymmetrical distribution of participation status by systematically withholding responses to physicians' announcements of their diagnoses. The announcement of diagnosis in the general practice consultation amounts to an 'informing', passed from the expert standpoint of the physician to the lay standpoint of the patient, about some aspect of the patient's physical condition. While, again, there is no institutionalised rule constraining patients from producing substantive responses to these informings, Heath showed that patients routinely react to the announcement of diagnosis either with silence or else by producing a downward-intoned grunt or 'yeh'. These withholdings of response occur even in cases where 'the doctor provides an opportunity for the patient to respond to the informing by not only delivering the diagnostic information within a distinct utterance or turn at talk, but also by leaving a gap following the medical assessment in which the patient has an extended possibility to reply' (Heath 1992: 240). Heath suggested that through this practice, patients tacitly act to sustain the asymmetrical dimensions of physician-patient interactions by ceding control over the encounter to the physician.

In research that has a closer connection with the present book, Peräkylä (1995) suggested that the emergent asymmetries found in his data of counselling sessions for (adult) patients taking an HIV test could be accounted for on the basis of a bricolage arrangement. The turn-taking itself is quasi-conversational, yet Peräkylä found emergent uniformities whereby counsellors tended either to ask questions, or produce post-response information statements directed at clients; while clients tended to restrict themselves to answering the questions put by counsellors. This pattern he accounted for not in terms of a normative specification of the relationship between the roles of counsellor and client and the activities of asking/informing, on the one hand, and answering on the other. For example, as Peräkylä (1995: 75–87) showed, when clients do ask questions this is not sanctioned or treated as a departure from the institutional norm by counsellors. Bricolage enables counsellors and clients to locally construct a pattern of turn-taking using stock conversational resources marshalled in the light of the particular circumstances of AIDS counselling.

A similar perspective underpins my analyses, in the following chapters, of how participants in child counselling sessions use bricolage practices to build locally managed regularities in turn-taking that render the talk both similar to ordinary conversation, yet recognisably specialised: in other words, quasi-conversational. The empirical topics I will address begin from the broad question of how child counsellors identify and draw out talk about therapeutic matters with the children whom they see. In addressing how counselling-relevant matters are topicalised using bricolage practices, I focus on specific aspects of a general feature of counselling talk in which counsellors 'pick up on' those aspects of the discourse environment—not just the words that are spoken, but also objects or circumstances that are implicated in what is said—which are open to being translated into 'therapeutic objects': that is, matters or issues in the client's everyday life that are amenable to some form of therapeutic intervention.

As we proceed, it will become clear how this work is necessarily accomplished through bricolage practices because counsellors cannot rely on norms and conventions to yield from children the kinds of turns necessary to get the work of counselling done. Rather, they rely partly on what they have learned from textbooks, from training and from practical experience about the kinds of turns that will best succeed in eliciting certain kinds of talk from the child; and partly on the essentially unpredictable contingencies of how each child responds to those turns with utterances of their own. In other words, the local management of child counselling talk is something that occurs in local sequential environments; and as in any form of talk-in-interaction, it is grounded in the participants' mutual orientation to the task at hand.

However, as we will see, children are not straightforwardly collaborative in the task-at-hand of child counselling. While, for the most part, children at least 'go along with' counsellors' attempts to have them talk about aspects of their family lives, they may be markedly resistant to revealing information about their feelings or concerns regarding ongoing family separations. This becomes a topic of particular attention in Chapter 6. But it is a situation that counsellors face, and have to find ways of dealing with, routinely. While textbooks can provide some guidance on ways of dealing with resistance (e.g. Geldard and Geldard 1998: 71–3), in naturally-occurring sessions counsellors need to marshall their resources in the here-and-now of unfolding talk. Bricolage, as the ad hoc moulding of interactional resources to hand, thus becomes especially useful in the management and maintenance of the institutional work of child counselling discourse.

CHAPTER 3

'So this is being taped'

From ethics to analytics in the data collection process

In line with the conversation analytic method, the data for this book consist of tape recordings of naturally occurring child counselling dialogues.[1] The original process of collecting that data was somewhat complex, since I had not only to identify a suitable and willing fieldsite, but also to gain 'informed consent' to the recording of sessions from potential participants. Initial contacts had been made with a major family therapy institute in order to facilitate data collection. Having expressed interest in principle in collaborating in the research, the practice in question underwent a change in management and the new Director was not prepared to pursue the collaboration further. Other organisations were then approached, including a national charitable foundation offering both family mediation and specialised child counselling.

After a number of meetings and discussions with counsellors and the Director, one of the foundation's London practices agreed to act as a field site. During the early stages of the project itself, other practices were contacted in other cities. Meetings were held in these places with managers and counsellors. Ultimately, however, the invitation to become involved in data collection was declined, usually for reasons to do with the sensitivity of the data to be recorded and concerns about confidentiality. For instance, it was often said that the counselling session was 'the child's space' and practitioners felt uneasy about allowing the researcher to have access to what went on in that space.

The practice where the data were eventually gathered offers counselling exclusively for children whose parents either have separated or are in the process of doing so. In a seven month period, recordings were made of fifteen complete sessions, including sessions conducted by both male and female counsellors, with both single children and siblings. In the latter cases, there are recordings of siblings seen by counsellors both together and separately. As already noted, the age range of the children is 4–12 years.

---

1. This chapter partially reproduces materials from an earlier publication, 'The moral status of technology: Being recorded, being heard and the construction of concerns in child counselling' in I. Hutchby and J. Moran-Ellis (eds.), *Children, Technology and Culture* (RoutledgeFalmer 2001).

Understandably, the staff of the practice shared my concern about gaining the informed consent of those willing to participate in the research; about ensuring the full confidentiality of the data (the recorded tapes); and about protecting the anonymity of the children. The counsellors, on whose cooperation the future of the research depended, expressed their preference for the researcher not to be present during counselling sessions, and they also expressed a preference to manage the gaining of consent from both parents and children themselves, in the context of the initial assessment meeting (it is for this reason that initial assessment meetings were not recorded).

After some discussion, we drew up a selection of consent forms: one designed for parents, and three others intended to explain the research in language accessible to children of varying age groups. These forms ensured full anonymity, gave the participants the right to withdraw consent at any time without prejudice, and sought to ensure confidentiality by restricting access to the audio tapes solely to the researcher. This latter policy was also intended to militate against the possibility of tapes being subpoenaed by lawyers acting for one or other parent in contested divorce proceedings. This was a possibility about which the Director of the practice, who was also experienced in mediation and in child protection procedure, expressed considerable concern. No recordings were undertaken unless one or both parents, and the child concerned, had signed the relevant consent form. Moreover, the identities of parents and children were withheld from the researcher, and tapes were labelled with client codes rather than children's names.

One consequence of this process was that during the data collection period, while the researcher was not physically present during recordings, the recording itself was not conducted covertly. The tape recorder was in full view of the participants throughout, the procedure being to place the device (a small battery operated portable machine) on a table at the side of the room, and situate two small, flat multidirectional microphones in different parts of the room (for example, one near the armchairs where participants would sit, and one near the toy cupboard from which children would choose games, often at the counsellor's invitation).

My aim in this chapter is to focus attention on this particular aspect of the talk: the fact that it involves a recording technology—the tape recorder and microphones—in clear visibility throughout the session. As we will see, counsellors were often concerned, particularly at the start of sessions, to render the technology's presence visible for the child, even though the fact that the session would be recorded (as well as the research purposes of the recording) had been discussed beforehand with both parents and children.

The issue I will discuss revolves around the role of the recording technology in the production of the talk; and, more particularly, the talk-instantiated work of the counselling session. Beginning from a concern, characteristic of much qualitative research, with naturalistic recording as an ethical issue, as well as one which possibly impacts on the 'authenticity' of what is being recorded, I offer an alternative focus on the fact of the recording as an analytic phenomenon. Looking at those moments where participants—both counsellor and child—display their orientations to the presence of the technology leads to a consideration of the ways in which the technology comes to have different forms of presence within the talk; and in which it is thus bound up with various aspects of the counselling session's distinctive interactional work.

From ethics to analytics

The tape-recording of discourse, especially in non-experimental or non-laboratory settings, brings with it a range of concerns, both ethical and analytical. On the ethical level, researchers need to decide whose consent among the participants should be sought prior to the recording taking place; and who among the relevant parties should be informed about the fact of the recording and the nature of the research. The general trend over recent years has been away from the use of 'covert' methods of data collection (for instance, using hidden recording devices, one-way mirrors and so forth), seeing these as deceptive and therefore unethical. Ethical standards in social research strongly favour the gaining of 'informed consent' from those whose participation is sought, or whose behaviour is to be recorded, prior to the initiation of data collection itself.

When young children are involved this ethical dimension takes on a greater salience. In this study, particularly in the light of legislation such as the UK Children Act of 1989 (one aim of which is to give children greater voice, agency and autonomy in terms of legal processes surrounding divorce), it was not thought appropriate simply to gain the consent of parents and counsellors to the recording of sessions. It was necessary also to gain the informed consent of children themselves. This was in accordance with guidelines issued by professional bodies such as the British Sociological Association and the British Psychological Society. The process of obtaining the informed consent of parents and children[2] was done prior to the counselling period actually starting, at the initial assessment meeting.

Aside from ethical issues of informed consent, however, the fact that both counsellor and child were fully cognisant of the presence of the tape recorder in the room also raises significant analytical issues. In social science, researchers working within

---

2. In legal terms, children under the age of majority may in fact only 'assent' to their parents' 'consent'; that is, children cannot overrule their parents' refusal of consent, though they can decline to give their own assent to something their parents have consented to.

both qualitative and quantitative paradigms have engaged in much methodological debate about the influence and effects of the researcher and their research instruments on the behaviour being investigated. 'Researcher effects', 'reactivity' or 'reactive effects' (Bryman 1988: 112; Hammersley 1992: 164; Hammersley and Atkinson 1995: 130), 'interviewer effects' (Fielding 1993: 145; Fowler and Mangione 1990: 46; Judd, Smith and Kidder 1991: 259), 'context effects' (Foddy 1993: 52ff), 'observer effects' (Robson 1993) and the 'observer's paradox' (Labov 1972) are just some of the terms used to describe the 'unintended' influence of the research technology and/or the researcher on the results of a study (Maykut and Moorhouse 1994: 155).

As Judd, Smith and Kidder (1991: 304–5) point out, participant observers tend to avoid recording conversations on tape because of a feeling that the recording device would 'inhibit the researcher's participation in many situations'. It may limit rapport and possibly 'interfere with participant observation'. Tape recording may also 'make respondents anxious' (Blaxter, Hughes and Tight 1996: 154). Hammersley and Atkinson (1983: 158) suggest that even where consent has been gained, 'awareness that proceedings are being recorded may significantly affect what occurs'. Stubbs (1983: 224) argues that ordinary speakers' language changes to a 'more formal' style when they know they are being observed. Ten Have (1999: 61) makes a related point, noting that 'even if people do consent to being recorded, they quite often offer nervously hilarious comments on possible exposures'. Thus, everyday language is 'susceptible to contamination by observation' (Stubbs 1983: 224). Since being tape-recorded and studied 'is not a normal situation for most people', there will always be the 'suspicion' that 'in extraordinary situations people produce extraordinary language' (ibid: 225).

In such methodological discussions, there is an implied realm of normal, natural and authentic social interaction that the presence of a researcher or of recording devices inevitably disturbs, distorts, or otherwise contaminates. 'Natural' interaction, it seems, could only be captured for research purposes if the researcher could stand behind a one-way mirror or become, in a literal sense, the proverbial fly-on-the-wall. This 'one-way mirror dilemma' (Speer and Hutchby 2003) represents a problem for research based on tape-recordings because, seen in this way, the ethically necessary procedures for recording social behaviour as it naturally occurs themselves lead to the distortion of the very phenomena to be analysed.

These issues are not confined to the methodological debates of social scientists. On a practical level, counsellors themselves were prone to express similar concerns during initial discussions about their involvement in the collection of data. For instance, would the presence of the recording device not have a detrimental effect by making it difficult to capture examples of 'authentic' counselling talk? Would it not prove problematic through inhibiting the child from speaking 'naturally'? And would it not, even, affect the counsellors themselves, making it difficult for them to produce the kind of talk they would 'normally' produce in a session? This is interesting partly because many counsellors and psychotherapists, particularly those in the field of family therapy (though not necessarily the ones involved in the present data[3]), routinely use one-way mirrors in their practice. The one-way mirror enables co-practitioners to observe the behavioural dynamics of clients without the possible distractions of being involved in direct interaction with the client. Yet presumably, the same concerns could be raised about the one-way mirror technique itself as were voiced about the presence of the tape recorder.

Concerns about 'natural' or 'authentic' talk are of particular significance, perhaps, when it comes to research in the area of conversation analysis. We have seen that CA relies for its data on the tape-recording of naturally-occurring talk-in-interaction. One upshot of this is that, in most cases, at least one of the participants whose talk is being recorded knows that a recording is taking place. That is, given the general reluctance of social researchers to conduct totally covert recording, there is an awareness at least for the participant operating the recording device, if not also for others involved in the interaction, that 'this interaction is being recorded'.

Unlike the researchers and counsellors referred to above, conversation analysts in general have not given much consideration to this factor or its potential significance. Despite the fact that large corpora of recorded telephone conversations have been gathered and transcribed, along with numerous collections of video recordings, one hardly ever finds in the literature any discussion of which participants, if any, were aware that a recording was being made or of the purposes for which it was intended. Among the reasons for this might be the way that CA's very basic commitment to working with tape-recorded materials developed. As Sacks described it in one of his earlier lectures:

> Such materials had a single virtue, that I could replay them. I could transcribe them somewhat and study them extendedly—however long it might take. The tape-recorded materials constituted a 'good enough' record of what had happened. Other things, to be sure, happened, but at least what was on the tape had happened. (Sacks 1984: 26)

This suggests an essentially pragmatic rationale: the tape is thought of primarily as a useful means of reproducing for repeated listening the detail of an actual event in the world, where the concern is not primarily with the 'completeness' or 'authenticity' of that event, but with what can be said about its achieved organisation as a piece of interaction. Thus, tape recording is often described in the CA literature as preferential to other standard data collection procedures, such as interviews, experiments, on-the-spot coding of behaviour, observation and the taking of fieldnotes. As Heritage and Atkinson (1984: 4) put it:

---

[3]. One counsellor did reveal that he had some experience, in another practice, of having sessions videorecorded for training purposes.

> the use of recorded data serves as a control on the limitations and fallibilities of intuition and recollection; it exposes the observer to a wide range of interactional materials and circumstances and also provides some guarantee that analytic conclusions will not arise as artifacts of intuitive idiosyncracy, selective attention or recollection, or experimental design.... [It] has the additional advantage of providing hearers and, to a lesser extent, readers of research reports with *direct* access to the data about which analytic claims are being made, thereby making them available for public scrutiny in a way that further minimises the influence of individual perceptions. (Emphasis in original)

However, conversation analysts (and some CA-influenced discourse analysts) have sometimes gone further than this, building a rhetorically effective distinction between 'natural' and 'contrived' data (Speer 2003a). Thus, one of the main issues in data collection has been to identify ways of gathering recordings that are as 'naturally occurring' as they can be. In Potter's (1996a: 135) description, natural data ideally comprise recordings of interaction 'that would have taken place ... in the form that it did, had the researcher not been born', while for ten Have (1999: 48), natural data is that which has not been 'co-produced with or provoked by the researcher' (see also Hutchby and Wooffitt 1998: 14). In such descriptions we see once again the shadow of the one-way mirror dilemma: it is easy to see how notions of 'informed consent' and overt data collection methods which make clearly visible the presence of a recording device can render these sorts of requirements problematic.

In one of the few discussions in the CA literature of the possible impacts of the presence of a recording technology, in this case a video camera, Drew (1989: 99–100) takes the following line of reasoning:

> Being filmed may indeed alter people's behaviour: it may make them nervous, they may make more jokes, talk more, be more withdrawn, sit in different places, hesitate to say certain things, and so on.... But if... the focus of one's analysis is... not on the frequency of some activity but on the details of its management and accomplishment, then any possible disturbance caused by participant's knowledge of their being filmed becomes unimportant. People cannot think about or control their behaviour at the level of detail for which the systematics of the organisation of action (verbal or non-verbal) are being investigated in conversation analysis.

This is a potentially controversial claim, especially in the sense that Drew makes his assertion about the levels at which people can 'think about or control their behaviour' without providing any supporting evidence. In fact, he is relying on a standard argument in conversation analysis, described in this way by Heritage and Atkinson (1984: 4):

> Conversation analytic researchers have come to an awareness that only the smallest fraction of what is used and relied on in interaction is available to unaided intuition. Conversation analytic studies are thus designed to achieve systematic analysis of what, at best, is intuitively known and, more commonly, is tacitly oriented to in ordinary conduct.

But the significant feature of Drew's claim for present purposes is that it implicitly proposes a level of 'authentic natural action' which can be analysed as such in spite of any potential impacts of the recording technology on the participants' behaviour. In other words, the 'systematics of the organisation of action' are seen as primordial: they necessarily underpin the production of mutually intelligible communication regardless of the context; and they transcend the psychological dispositions of individuals who may, at a higher level of awareness, be more or less affected by the presence of a recording technology.

Drew's approach therefore does not offer a solution to the problem posed by the one-way mirror dilemma. Instead it works to sidestep the issue by arguing that the phenomena of real interest are those that are tacitly oriented to in interaction. In doing so, it implicitly acknowledges the terms of the one-way mirror dilemma by positing a level of 'authentic' behaviour which cannot, in fact, be affected by the processes and techniques of data collection.

I want to argue that the conversation analytic perspective offers another—analytically more powerful—way of approaching the one-way mirror dilemma. Instead of attempting to solve it or find a way around it, this is to examine the ways in which the recording device is, in fact, observably oriented to—and thus made interactionally relevant—by the participants as the talk unfolds. Instead of seeing the presence of a recording device as potentially contaminating what would otherwise be a pristine occasion of real-world interaction, and rather than worrying over the extent to which participants' noticing of, making reference to, or otherwise displaying orientations to the fact of their being recorded gets in the way of the 'authentic' talk that is to be analysed, we should instead concentrate on investigating precisely what it is that participants are doing when they orient to being recorded. In particular, how might what they do in such orientations play a part in the ongoing construction of specific situated interactions?

Therefore, this approach represents a different perspective on the process of recording-based social research than that which generates the one-way mirror dilemma in the first place. From this perspective, it is not the case that the presence of a recording device—or even a researcher—makes the occasion somehow 'nonnatural'. Neither does an observable orientation by participants to a tape recorder or a researcher's presence mean that such orientations contaminate the phenomena or render (some aspect of) the interaction 'inauthentic'.

The phrase 'from ethics to analytics' is intended to convey a shift from an ethical concern with informed consent to the overt recording of talk, to an analytical concern with what is done in that talk when the fact of the recording is topicalised by the participants. This means asking what role the technological device itself might play in the unfolding of the session. Do participants appear to orient to its significance in any observable ways? And if so, what are the ways in which the technology itself comes to impinge on the work of the counselling session: on the aim to have the child verbalise and explore his or her feelings about a problematic life situation (Geldard and Geldard 1997)? Is the presence of the recording technology inherently problematic; or might there be ways in which its presence can have an enabling effect?

In what follows I present some observations which illustrate the analytical pay-offs from adopting such a methodological stance. The main focus is on one particular session with an eight year old child in which, at the very start of the session, the tape recorder was accorded various statuses by both participants. As we will see, the attribution of presence, both physical and, in some sense, moral, to the technological device is not to be seen as a negative feature of the counselling session. Rather, it turns out to facilitate a wide range of talk about the child's responses to the breakdown of her parents' relationship. What I will show is a range of ways that the counsellor monitors, interprets and constructs the child's utterances in order to bring into play possible 'concerns' about family relationships. Orientations to the technology play a part in this, as the presence of the tape recorder comes to be situated within three interrelated interpretive frameworks: 'being recorded', 'being heard', and 'being counselled'. These frames colour the interpretation of utterances at different points in the opening stages of the session in question.

Observability: 'Being recorded'

'Jenny' is an eight-year-old child whose parents have brought her to the service because they are currently in the process of negotiating a separation. Jenny saw the (male) counsellor on four occasions. My observations will focus on the first full session (the 'post-assessment' session). At various points in this session (not only at its beginning), both the counsellor and the child displayed their orientations to the presence, and the relevance, of the tape recorder and associated technological phenomena (the microphones, the reels, volume controls, LCD sound level monitor, etc.). Thus, the presence of the technology becomes *observable* from the participants' points of view.

There is a significant distinction between orienting to the 'presence' of the technology and orienting to its 'relevance'. Orienting to the presence of the device means according it a status as a physical object within the room. This may involve a variety of actions; for instance, mentioning that there is a tape recorder on the table, noticing aspects of it such as the flashing LCD lights on its recording display, asking questions about how certain aspects of it operate, and so on. Orienting to the device's relevance, on the other hand, means bringing its presence into play in situations where it may not be overtly oriented to in the first sense, but where it is taken by one or other participant to be implicated somehow in what is being said. Both these means of orienting to the technology are involved in the counsellor's work of enabling the child to speak about her feelings; and both will be illustrated in the course of the analysis.

The first mention of the device's presence comes right at the beginning of the session, as the counsellor and the child are engaged in selecting the places where each will sit:

(1) C19/99: 1a
```
 1 → C:  Sit down and we'll ta:lk about the recording >(if you
 2        like) f'r a< mo:ment, (.) Where you gonna sit. >Djwanna
 3        sit?< (.) Sit over there.
 4        (2.2) ((Sound of footsteps))
 5    C:  Oowuhhh (.) Where shall I sit. (0.2) Shall I
 6        si[t  over] here,
 7    J:     [There.]
 8    J:  No there. There.
 9    C:  Which one this one o[ver he]re?=
10    J:                      [There.]   =Yeah.
11    C:  Right. (.) Okay. (1.5) Oowhhhh (0.5) So yeah. Djwan- (.)
12        If yer feeling uncomfortable, take your bag off won't
13        you.(0.3) If you want to: or leave it on you decide.
14        (3.1) ((Rustling sounds))
15    C:  So:. hhh .hh (.) So your second time he:re,
16        (3.6)
17    C:  Yeah? .thhh So an-and (.) ((banging)) I'm gonna move the
18        chair cuz I- (0.4) ca:n't see you very well. .h I's too
19        far away.
20        ((Banging))
21    J:  Hunh hee he he
22    C:  Hhh .h ((sniff)) So've [you-
23 → J:                          [So this is being recorded.
```

As they enter the room C mentions 'the recording' (line 1) and suggests that, if the child likes, they can 'ta:lk about' it. What immediately follows this, however, is not talk about the recording but a discussion about (a) where J might like to sit, and (b) where C should sit, the latter issue being resolved by J herself (lines 7–10). The ensuing few turns involve a series of five attempts by C to initiate the session proper, each of them using the prefatory item 'So': 'So yeah' (line 11), 'So:', 'So your second time he:re' (both line 15), 'So an- and' (line 17); ultimately moving towards the production of a first question for the child: 'So 've you-' (line 22). This question is interrupted by J herself reintroducing the issue of the recording: 'So this is being recorded.' (line 23).

There are a number of points to note about this initial sequence. First, J displays her orientation to the relevance of the recording device by picking up on C's first brief mention, even though subsequently C gives indications that he may be moving away from that topic. His attempts to initiate the session instead involve references to this as the 'second time' (i.e. the first post-assessment session), and the beginnings of a question taking the form 'So [ha]ve you . . .'. Neither of these give any clear indication that the recording is about to be topicalised. Rather, the impression is that it is the session itself, and perhaps some issues connecting back to the first assessment, that will be the initial topic of talk. C may, of course, have good reasons for not wanting to make too much of the presence of the recording device, given counsellors' above mentioned concerns about normalcy and naturalness in the session.

Second, J's reintroduction of the topic itself utilises the very prefatory marker 'So' used five times already by C: 'So this is being recorded.' This suggests that she may have been monitoring C's aborted attempts to produce a 'So'-prefaced sentence in the light of an expectation that these would, indeed, eventually result in an opportunity to 'ta:lk about the recording'. Having heard the counsellor's initial move away from that topic, with 'So your second time he:re,' (line 15), and then heard the beginnings of his second apparent shift, the start of the question 'So 've you-' (line 22), J comes in with her own proposed completion of the sentence: 'So this is being recorded.'

The third point is that this of course involves J, an eight year old child, taking the initiative (in the sense of taking control of the topic and, therefore, the immediate course of the session) in a discourse environment where it might be expected that the adult (a professional child counsellor) would do that. This is not meant as a negative reflection of this particular counsellor's skills. Far from it: as we will see, he is able to turn the child's displayed orientations to the presence and relevance of the recording device to good therapeutic use. It is rather to note something else: namely the fact that it is the very presence of the device that comes to furnish the environment in which the child can engage in this initiative-taking move. In other (non-recorded) circumstances, there may be other features of the environment which a child may draw upon in order to initiate their own line of interaction. The point with this datum is that the recording technology is shown to have something more than a mere constraining effect on the course of the talk. Even at this early stage in the session, and in this relatively minor way, the device begins to reveal its affordances as a resource for the (child's) initiation of a course of action.

Extract (2) shows how this course of action proceeds:

(2) C19/99: 1a   ((Continuation of extract 1))
    22   C: Hhh .h ((sniff)) So've [you-
    23   J.   [So this is being recorded.
    24   C: This is being re↓corded now.
    25   J: ((brightly)) ↑O:ka::y,
    26   C: Yeah.
    27   J: I sound like a ba:by.
    29   (.)
    30   C: Are you worried that you sound like a baby,
    31   (.)
    32   J: No↑::,=
    33   C: Or dju think sounding like a baby's oka[y.
    34   J: [(Dae)
    35   c↑a:↓r:e=ehh
    36   C: Yeah? heh .h Who=who thinks you sound like a baby most.
    37   (0.7)
    38   J: My grandma an' grandad.
    39   C: De- An' what does s:he say tuh- to tell you that she
    40   thinks you sound like a baby.
    41   J: You sound like a ↑baby.
    42   C: Does she. (0.2) .hh An' dju think she:- she l- does she
    43   ↑like that or, (.) d[oes she sa]:y, that she's not- not=
    44   J: [(   )]
    45   C: =liking it.
    46   J: She doesn't like it cuz I say it sounds like my cousin.
    47   C: A:hh
    48   J: Eh huh huh hee heuh .u .hh

C responds to J's topicalisation of the recording by confirming that the session is indeed being recorded (line 24), after which J utters 'O:ka::y' with a playfully exaggerated brightness. What happens next illustrates another way in which the technology's presence, having been mentioned, is brought to bear on a course of action: this time, an entry into a therapeutic dialogue.

J's next comment, 'I sound like a ba:by' (line 27), is hearable in a number of different ways. For instance, it may be taken to be an expression of her self-consciousness about being recorded; or we might imagine that this is something she has either been told or decided herself on occasions when she may have been playing with recording her voice on a tape recorder. From a conversation analytic perspective, however, what is of most relevance is the understanding or interpretation that her interlocutor, the counsellor, displays of this utterance in his following turn in the sequence.

Of the many and varied ways in which anyone might respond to an eight year old child's announcement that 'I sound like a ba:by' (for example, 'Do you?', 'No you don't', 'Who says that?', 'Why do you think that?', 'What's wrong with that?', etc.), C selects one that begins quite clearly to frame the sequence up in therapeutic terms: 'Are you worried that you sound like a baby'. The significance of this is that it manifests an orientation to the child's talk as involving 'concerns'. More than that: it constructs J's utterance as one that may be expressive of a concern. In picking up on a hearing of the assertion 'I sound like a ba:by' that treats it as possibly expressive of a concern, rather than (for example) a factual observation, C is engaged in making relevant a counselling 'frame' for the present interaction. It is not clear, on the surface of things, whether J's turn in line 27 shows her to be oriented to the relevance of 'counselling' rather than (or in addition to) that of 'being recorded'. But C's response in line 29 clearly seeks to bring that relevance to bear on the talk.

Here, then, is a second way in which displayed orientations to the presence of the technological device can be recruited in the pursuit of other interactional projects relevant to the setting. By 'hearing' the child's reference to what she sounds like not simply within the frame of reference of 'being recorded', but also that of 'being counselled', the counsellor is able to direct the talk towards providing a first picture of J's relationship with family members (in this case, her grandparents).

There are other frames of reference which can be brought to bear upon orientations to the technology's presence. One of the most significant, itself related in different ways to the frames of 'being recorded' and 'being counselled', is that of 'being heard'.

Analysability: 'Being heard' and the moral status of the technology

The next extract shows how the counsellor's picture of the child's possible concerns about her family relationships becomes filled out quite substantially, again by means of displayed orientations to the technology's presence. What is of note here is the way that the discourse moves between the relevancies not just of counselling and 'being recorded', but also of a third possible framework: 'being heard'. Notice how, in the course of the extract, the counsellor once again orients to aspects of the child's actions in respect of the tape recorder as possibly expressive of concerns, and how the technology and features of its layout (recall that there are two microphones placed in different parts of the room) come to stand in for moral evaluations of J's relationships with her two parents.

(3) C:19: 99: 1a
1   C: So:::, (0.8) as you say Jenny i' is being recorded, (0.4)
2   an' look there's a microphone ther:e,
3   J: Boo(h)↓oo: uhih hi[h hee h*eh
4   C: [uheh
5   C: An' another one, (.) the other side of the roo:m,
6   (.)
7   J: Let's see. ((Footsteps))
8   C: Can you see it,
9   (3.2)
10   J: ((Close to microphone)) Oh ye:::ah.
11   C: Yeah?=
12   J: =That one can't record as much because we're over here.
13   C: Yeh I guess so.
14   (1.5)
15   C: So d'you think this microphone's gonna record us more
16   than the other one.
17   J: Yeah.
18   (3.0)
19   C: [[Wu-
20   J: [[Cuz, if we speak really loudly that one will be able to
21   get it.
22   C: °Yee:ah. (.) Guess so.°
23   (1.6)
24 → J: He↑LLO:::::! hee hinh=
25   C: =Djthink that microphone heard that.
26   (1.8)
27   C: No:.
28 → J: .hhh↑HE↑↑LLO:::::! (0.4) Think it heard that.
29   (3.2)
30 → C: .hhh How l:oud dyou have t' speak at ho:me. .h t'get
31   people to hear you.
32 → J: .hh Well my ↑da:d's: ↓de:af.
33   (0.4)
34   C: ↑A:↓h:.
35   J: So I >have t'go-< .h (.) This morning I w' trying to get
36   his attention cuz I saw something in a magazine that I
37   might want, .hhh an', I'm goin', ↑DA:↓:D, knock ↑knO:↓CK,
38   are you ↑thE:::↓RE, (.)↑DA:↓:D, ↑DA:↓:(h)D!hhh
39   (0.8)

```
40    C:  An' did 'e hear.
41    J:  No.
42    C:  Not at a:ll.
43    J:  No:.
44        (1.2)
45    C:  Okay. (.) .hhhh So how d'you get his attention.
46        (0.6)
47    J:  I have to gettuh up an' go an' (.) sort of like
48        s:strangle ehhih(m) (.) .hh ba:sic'lly:, (1.6) Kick him
49        or somethi[ng.
50    C:            [What abou:t (.) getting your mum t'hear what
51        you've got to s[ay.
52 →  J:                [°She hears everything.°=
53    C:  =Mum hears absolutely everything.
54    J:  °°Yeh°°
```

In an incremental, turn by turn development, aspects of the geography of the technology here lead into a discussion of the child's picture of her problematic home life. The key to this is again the counsellor's orientation to 'counselling' in addition to 'being recorded', in his question at line 30–1. Once more, this involves a hearing of J's hails aimed at the differently located microphones—'Boo(h)↓oo:' in line 3, and 'He↑LLO:::::!' (line 24) followed by an even louder '.hhh↑HE↑↑LLO:::::!' in line 28—as possibly expressive of concerns: in this case, a concern about 'being heard at home'.

The main image associated with C's question 'How l:oud dyou have t' speak at ho:me' (line 30) is a common one used in child counselling and in books aimed at helping children 'get through' parental separation—that of parents continually arguing and children being made to feel miserable in the middle. Yet the very mention of this stock image in counselling at this particular point in the session seems to emerge out of clearly displayed orientations to the presence of the technology. More than that, there is a sense in which the discussion of the two microphones (one quite close by, the other on the opposite side of the room) and the subsequent discussion of the child's communicative relationship with her parents (one who often does not hear her, the other who hears everything) reflect one another.

Note that 'hearing' is a concept introduced in this exchange by the counsellor (in line 25) and subsequently picked up by the child (in line 28). The child herself had initially used a more mechanical vocabulary in referring to the microphones: 'That one can't record as much' (line 12). Later she uses a slightly different term: 'If we speak really loudly that one will be able to get it' (line 20), and it might be said that 'get it' occupies a kind of intermediate status between the mechanical, inanimate 'record' and the far more animate, anthropomorphic 'hear' used by the counsellor. But the use of 'hear' in relation to the microphones is interesting because, in as much as it is taken up by J in line 28 ('think it heard that one'), it links into the subsequent exchange about the hearing of her parents.

Note, then, the close relationship between the way J describes her father and mother's 'hearing' of her and the way the differently located microphones have been mentioned. She asserts (in line 32) that her father is 'deaf' (though it is not clear that this is the case, especially since C, who has met the father, responds by orienting to this as 'news' as opposed to merely acknowledging what should be a mutually shared piece of knowledge), and that she has to yell at him to get his attention (lines 35–8). It is interesting to note that there is a close prosodic match between J's enunciation of 'He↑LLO:::::!' (line 24) and '.hhh↑HE↑↑LLO:::::!' (line 28), and '↑DA:↓:D, knock ↑knO:↓CK, are you ↑thE::↓RE, (.)↑DA:↓:D, ↑DA:↓:(h)D!hhh' (line 37–8). The first set of hails has a 'singsong' prosody which is reproduced in a more pronounced way in the second set. Although difficult to capture in the form of a transcript, in the hearing this makes for a markedly close link between the (here-and-now) address to the microphone and the (reported) address to the father.

There is also an intriguing relationship between the description of the mother (in line 52) and the previous discussion of the recording microphones. Invited to draw a comparison between the necessary actions in getting her father's attention and those involved in gaining her mother's, J announces, with a marked drop in volume, that her mother 'hears everything'. And when C invites a confirmation, with 'Mum hears absolutely everything' (line 53), J responds by dropping her voice almost to a whisper: '°°Yeh°°' (line 54).

Although there is no clear indication that the child is consciously making these comparisons between the different aural capacities of the two microphones and those of her two parents, the link is a striking one, particularly when we bear in mind the close sequential and temporal relationship between the respective descriptions of 'hearing' and 'being heard'. What is clear, nevertheless, is that the counsellor's introduction of the topic of 'being heard at home', on which the comparison turns, has a direct sequential link to the child's utterance in the turn that precedes it, where she refers to the microphone having 'heard that'. Again, albeit in a more ambivalent way, we can trace a relationship between orientations to the technology's presence and the production of a counselling frame for the talk.

In the following case, we see another example of the counsellor picking up on references which may orient to the technology's relevance (as distinct from merely its presence), and using that to lead the child into talk about 'concerns'. The issue here hinges on different aspects of 'hearing' and 'being heard'. It is somewhat later in the session, and the child is drawing pictures, the counsellor exploring with her some thoughts about these pictures. J has drawn a sketch of a dog, which she describes as 'very thin' and as 'a stray'. This comes to initiate a lengthy story involving many other drawings. I will just focus on the beginning stage of this story.

(4) C:19:99:1c
```
   1    C:   It's good to pretend sometimes.
   2    J:   .h Well ACtually he was locked in a boot an' he got out,
   3         (0.3) an' and the r-RSPCA found 'im 'n 'e, .hh he- .h
   4         h[e-
   5    C:   [He w'z locked in someone's boot?
   6         (0.4)
   7    C:   Goodn[ess.
   8→  J:         [Y- The RSPCA found him, .hh[h He was] on TV=
   9    C:                                    [Uh huh. ]
  10    J:   =en he ran away=.h=an' 'e couldn't find a home.
  11         (0.8)
  12    C:   So:: he- did 'e=who did 'e run away from the boot or from
  13         the RSPCA.
  14         (0.3)
  15    J:   The RSPCA[:.
  16    C:            [He ran away-=
  17→  J:   =Cuz 'e was scared of the camera.
```

Note here two things in particular. First, J's utterance in line 8, 'He was on TV'; and second, her remark that the dog ran away 'cuz 'e was scared of the camera' (line 17). It is not clear whether these references, at the moment of production, are associated with J's orientation to the actual presence of a different kind of recording technology in the room at present. However, the next extract shows how, as the story carries on, the counsellor indeed picks up on this very possibility (note especially line 22, and lines 24–6):

(5) C:19:99:1c   ((Continuation of extract 4))
```
  17    J:   Cuz 'e was scared of the camera.
  18         (.)
  19    C:   So the people that were tryin' to- (.) help 'im, he ran
  20         away from.
  21         (1.1)
  22→  C:   He was scared of th'camera.
  23         (0.7)
  24→  C:   .h Dju think 'e would've been sca:red, .hh if there was
  25         no camera. (.) But if hi:s voice was being taped but not
  26         being filmed?
```

```
27    J:  mYeah.
28    C:  He'd've still been scared then,
29    J:  °Mm:.°
30        (0.2)
31    C:  A:h.
32        (2.8)
33    C:  How could=how could he not be sca:red, (0.2) with his
34        voice being taped.
35        (1.9)
36    J:  Wull, if:: he::, (0.3) yihsee he's got very good hearing.
37    C:  Ye:ah,
38        (.)
39    J:  mYeh.
40        (0.5)
41    J:  An' so[:
42    C:        [Bit like your mum.
43        (0.6)
44    J:  Yeah. .h[h      ] An'::, (0.4) so::.
45    C:          [Mm.]
46        (1.7)
47    C:  What=what does that mean having good hearing.
48        (0.9)
49 →  J:  He can hear the tape recorder goin', bvhvh[vhv
50    C:                                            [He c'n hear it
51        whirling round.=
52    J:  =Yeah.
```

We again find the counsellor orienting to the child's utterances as possibly expressive of concerns, except that this time, references to the technology are not to be heard in terms of concerns about 'being heard' within the family situation. Rather, the concern is taken to be about the fact of 'being recorded' within the counselling session itself.

The pivotal utterance here is in lines 24–6, where C renders explicit a relationship that is only potentially present in the child's remarks about the stray dog's fear of 'the camera': that is, the relationship between this fictionalised event and the child's current circumstance. More than that, C's turn invites J herself to see, and to go along with, that proposed relationship. As the exchange proceeds, it becomes ambivalent as to whether it is the imagined concerns or fears of the dog, or the real concerns of the child, that are at issue (note the continued third person reference in the child's turns in lines 36 and 49). This ambivalence is shown especially clearly in the child's turn in line 49, in which she mimics the muted sound of the actually present tape recorder in the course of describing how the dog's fears arise because of the fact that 'he's got very good hearing' (line 36). Once again, then, 'hearing' and 'being heard' are brought up as central concerns, this time in the context of a story where the concerns of a fictional character become merged with the supposed concerns of the child storyteller.

In these examples it has become clear that the technology may not be oriented to simply as a presence in the room, but more significantly, in terms of its relevance for the activities being carried out within the room. In the process, the inanimate objects of tape recorder and (differently located) microphones come to be attributed with a range of complex identities, linked to which are a number of moral statuses. In the course of the talk, the relevance of 'being recorded' interweaves with that of 'counselling' and 'expressing concerns', 'hearing' and 'being heard', and the status of the technology shifts as it is used to facilitate forms of counselling talk.

Conclusion

There are those among the community of social researchers, as well as among the communities of socially researched (such as professional counsellors), for whom the presence of a recording device as a data collection technology renders problematic the 'normalcy', 'naturalness' and 'authenticity' of the events and actions being recorded. This tends to be expressed in the form of a view that participants' awareness of the fact that they are being recorded will alter their behaviour, such that the researcher's object of analysis is inevitably distorted. Given contemporary ethical standards challenging the conduct of covert data collection, particularly when it involves children or those from disadvantaged groups, such a concern raises serious questions about the viability of qualitative research based on naturalistic data.

These concerns about the authentic, the natural and the normal are often at the heart of methodological considerations in counselling psychology, much of which is directed towards evaluation of the counselling process or of counselling outcomes (see Woolfe and Dryden 1996). Silverman (1996) observes how a vast amount of counselling research seeks to develop a normative model of good counselling practice which can be assessed using either quantitative measures of 'outcomes' or qualitative measures of people's 'responses' to counselling. However, each of these emphases in different ways leads to a situation in which the phenomenon itself—that is, what actually happens in the counselling session—disappears. In order to keep that phenomenon squarely in view, we have to turn the focus not towards what people think *about* counselling but towards what they *do* in counselling. The aim, therefore, is not to begin with a normative model of counselling which the presence of the tape recorder may in some sense distort. Rather, by focusing on events within the counselling session as it unfolds, a conversation analytic approach turns the question about the possible 'effect' of the recording on the 'reality' of the session into a different issue: one which asks, what kind of presence (if any) does the tape recorder have in terms of the observable behaviour of the participants, both counsellor and child?

Rather than assuming—and worrying—that the data is inevitably distorted due to the presence of a recording technology, one thing we can do is to turn the technology's presence into an analytical phenomenon. The fact that participants in the data presented above explicitly orient to the presence and the relevance of the technology does not mean that their interaction is not 'authentic'. Certainly, had the recording device not been there, they might not have engaged in some of the talk reproduced above. But this is an interactional event involving a tape recorder; just as, on a different day, there may have been a training practitioner present as an observer, and that in its turn would have been analysable as an interactional event involving a non-participating observer. In either case, it is the event as it unfolds that is of analytic interest, rather than some 'real thing' that would 'otherwise' have taken place.

In treating the technology's presence as an analytic phenomenon, we have seen how the participants themselves observably orient to it as an interactional phenomenon. But more than that, it is clear that the device, far from simply 'standing in the way' of the setting's activities, becomes actively bound up with those activities through the very orientations of the participants. Instead of being a determinate negative force, the technology reveals a whole array of communicative affordances (Hutchby 2001) which enable both the counsellor and the child to begin communicating about the (largely implicit) matter at hand: the estrangement of the child's parents. Apart from instigating talk about what the child has been told, by adults, that she 'sounds like', the technology in its particular spatial configuration affords the child an imagined comparison with her differential relationship with her father and mother. Similarly, the audible hum of the reels affords incorporation into the imagined dilemmas of the fictional characters she invents in the course of a story. Out of these affordances, as we have seen, the counsellor is able to begin, sometimes tentatively and sometimes leadingly, to constitute a therapeutic object.

CHAPTER 4

Talking about feelings

The perspective-display series in child counselling

It is a general feature of counselling that the practice depends for its success on the collaborative production of talk about 'therapeutic objects': particular concerns, feelings, worries or difficulties the client is experiencing and that furnish a reason for him or her being in counselling. The type of interventions that may result from such talk range from specific recommendations as to what a client may do in order to change or ameliorate a situation that has been identified as problematic, to much vaguer procedures such as drawing the client's attention to linkages between different circumstances that may be implicated in the problem. But wherever the intervention lies along this continuum, its production depends on the prior identification of a therapeutic object to which it can act as a response.

This process of topicalising possible concerns involves what I will call therapeutic vision: the ability, as part of the professional and institutional work of doing counselling, to identify and work up the existence of issues that are amenable to a counselling intervention. In child counselling, this can be complex because children are often reluctant to volunteer the kinds of concerns, or talk about feelings ('feelings-talk') that counsellors, in their professional role, desire to elicit. Certainly, we do not find young children entering the setting prepared to 'put issues on the table' for discussion, in the way that counsellors and psychotherapists dealing with adults (particularly in private work with paying clients) are wont to expect (Pain 2003).

There are two significant factors at work here that are similar to themes that have previously been drawn out by Peräkylä (1995) in his work on AIDS counselling for adults—another environment where counsellors regularly encounter difficulties in topicalising therapeutic objects. First of all, in both settings there is an 'opacity of frame', in the sense that 'what the general goals of a counselling session are may be more or less opaque' (Peräkylä 1995: 98). This might, in fact, be characteristic of counselling in general, since:

> There is no shared public understanding concerning what counselling…is about. We—as ordinary members of Western societies—do not know what happens in counselling with the same precision as we know what is going on in a doctor's surgery or in a lecture hall.   (Peräkylä 1995: 98)

The second factor is the overarching presence of 'delicate topics' in both child counselling and AIDS counselling dialogues. As Peräkylä (1995: 100) writes about his own data:

> During much of the time in counselling sessions, the participants are talking about the clients' sexual practices and about their fears concerning the future. The etiquette of addressing topics like these is very complex in ordinary conversation (cf. Jefferson 1980). The counsellors, however, direct the talk—sometimes persistently—towards these issues [while clients] talk about delicate matters only as much as counsellors, through their questions, create special space for such talk.

These factors are equally salient—albeit in somewhat different ways—in the child counselling setting. In terms of the 'opacity of frame', children have often been brought to the practice at their parents' behest and for reasons that the parents treat as important. For instance, perhaps their behaviour in reaction to the parents' separation is seen as problematic; or perhaps the parents simply want their child to be given the opportunity to explore their feelings about the situation with someone external to the family. There is therefore no guarantee that children will come to the sessions with any shared investment in the process and its intended goals and outcomes.

At the same time, the topics under discussion are, as in Peräkylä's (1995) data, 'delicate'. The reason for the child entering the counselling session in the first place, in these particular cases, is that their parents either have separated or are in the process of doing so. The main topic under discussion, therefore, is the break-up of a family unit and the worries or concerns that the child has in relation to that event. As noted above, children do not tend to volunteer specific information on their worries or concerns; however counsellors nonetheless work on the assumption that such concerns exist and 'direct the talk—sometimes persistently—towards these issues' (Peräkylä 1995: 100). Therefore counsellors work up interpretations of children's talk and other activities that favour the possibility that the child may be 'angry', 'confused', 'upset', and so forth.

We saw some signs of this in Chapter 3. There, although the child in question was talkative and collaborated with the counsellor in discussion about a variety of topics, the bulk of the work involved in linking the child's utterances to possible therapeutic concerns was done by the counsellor. We saw the counsellor's therapeutic vision in the way that he picked up on aspects of the discourse environment—not just the words that were spoken, but also objects or circumstances that were implicated in what was said—in such a way as to translate them into therapeutic objects.

In this chapter I discuss a particular type of sequence that occurs frequently in my data and by which counsellors seek to exercise this kind of therapeutic vision. It is similar to what Maynard (1989, 1991) called the perspective-display series in which one participant in talk-in-interaction seeks another's position, viewpoint or understanding in relation to a topic. Typically, the viewpoint that is expressed is then compared with or related to the first speaker's own view, and Maynard shows how such a sequence is used to perform varieties of interactional work in ordinary conversation and certain institutional settings.

I begin by outlining in more detail Maynard's (1991) account of the perspective-display series in both ordinary conversation and medical interactions, before examining how a similar technique functions somewhat differently in the child counselling setting. The key point is that while the perspective-display series succeeds in enabling certain interactional work to be done in both conversation and medical consultation, it does not appear to succeed when deployed in the child counselling setting. The reasons for this tell us more about the nature of child counselling as institutional interaction.

The perspective-display series

As Maynard (1991) observes, numerous strategies exist in everyday conversation by which a participant can give an opinion or assessment. One such strategy is simply to offer the opinion at an opportune moment in the unfolding interaction. Frequently, as Pomerantz (1984) shows, such offers of opinions or assessments are treated by their recipient as occasioning a 'second assessment' (i.e., one of their own) in the next turn. But another strategy is for one party first to solicit the other's opinion, then produce an opinion of his or her own which takes the first opinion into account. This—the perspective-display series, or PDS—is a strategy that seems to be used in contexts where there is a desire for agreement or congruency between opinions.

Consider the following example from an exchange involving two teenagers talking about certain types of wheels used in customising cars:

(1) From Maynard 1991: 459
```
 1→ Bob:   Have you ever heard anything about wire wheels?
 2→ Al:    They can be a real pain. They you know they go outta line
 3         and-
 4→ Bob:   Yeah the- if ya get a flat you hafta take it to a special
 5         place ta get the flat repaired.
 6→ Al:    Uh—why's that?
 7    Bob: Cause um they're really easy to break. I mean to bend
 8         and damage.
 9→ Al:    Oh really?
10    Bob: An' (.) most people won' touch 'em unless they 'ave the
11         special you know equipment or they- they have the know
12         how.
```

	13	Al:	They're like about two hundred bucks apiece or something
	14		too.
	15	Bob:	Yeah, ya get 'em- you get 'em chromed and that's the only
	16		way to have 'em just about too you know.
	17	Al:	heh Yeah

In line 1, Bob solicits a perspective on 'wire wheels': a type of wheel which his coparticipant, as a fellow car customiser or would-be 'hotrodder', may be taken to have a similar kind of awareness of, if not an actual opinion about. Line 2 shows that Al indeed has that awareness; but more than that, he treats Bob's solicitation as an occasion to give his opinion on wire wheels—that they 'can be a real pain'. As he proceeds to expand on that negative assessment, Bob comes in with an agreement followed by his own negative assessment of wire wheels (that flat tyres cannot be repaired by hand but have to be taken to 'a special place'). Following this, there are turns in which Al topicalises Bob's negative assessment (in lines 6 and 9), after which the pair of them continue on with other notable downsides to wire wheels (you need special equipment, they are expensive, they are only acceptable to the hotrodding community if chromed, and so on).

This extract is an exemplar of the PDS as found in ordinary conversation, which can be represented in formal terms in the following way:

The perspective-display series in conversation
1. A solicits B's perspective
2. B produces perspective
3. A produces own perspective, taking account of B's
4. B topicalises A's perspective

As Maynard (1991: 466) notes, the first move in the series,[1] a perspective-display invitation, operates to open an interactional context which 'allows one party to deliver reports and make assessments of social objects in a way that is sensitive to another party's understanding or perspective and to simultaneously provide for a favourable response to the delivered report'.

Significantly, however, Maynard also notes that:

> A search through a variety of conversational collections turned up fewer instances of this series among *acquainted* than among *unacquainted* parties. It may be that the circuitous way in which the PDS allows arrival at a third-turn 'report' is an inherently cautious maneouvre that makes the series particularly adaptable to environments

---

1. The PDS tends to be described, as here, in terms of slots in an unfolding sequential pattern. Hence, it may or may not be the case that any specific PDS comprises four 'actual' turns or more (though it could not consist of fewer than four); but in any given case the series is produced by means of the actions represented here occurring in their slots and in this order.

of professional-lay interaction, conversations among unacquainted parties, and so on. (Maynard 1991: 460; original emphasis)

For this reason, Maynard quickly turns to a more detailed examination of the perspective-display series in non-conversational discourse; specifically, clinical interactions between pediatricians and the parents of young children who potentially have developmental problems and about whom a diagnosis is about to be announced. In other words, like counselling dialogues, these are interactions characterised by the introduction of 'delicate' topics: namely information about a young child's degree of mental retardation, linguistic impairment, and so on.

It turns out that clinicians in this context frequently issue perspective-display invitations to parents prior to their announcement of a diagnosis. Such invitations ask for the parents' own opinion on what is 'wrong' with their child or what they see as the 'problem':

(2) From Maynard 1991: 468
1   Dr E: What do you see? as- his difficulty.
2   Mrs C: Mainly his uhm- the fact that he doesn't understand
3   everything and also the fact that his speech is
4   very hard to understand what he's saying, lots of
5   time

(3) From Maynard 1991: 469
1   Dr E: Wu- whatta you think his PRObIem is
2   Mrs M: Speech

(4) From Maynard 1991: 474
1   Dr S: Now that you've- we've been through all this I
2   just wanted to know from YOU. HOW you see J at this
3   time.
4   Mrs C: The same.
5   Dr S: Which is?
6   Mrs C: Uhm she can't talk.

Note that these extracts are not taken from the start of the initial consultation period. Rather, in each case, the doctor already has the clinical diagnosis 'in hand' but is delaying announcing that diagnosis in favour of asking for the parent's own viewpoint first. Maynard (1991) suggests that the reason for this is that it enables the doctor to create an environment in which the eventual diagnosis—which may contain quite devastating news about a child's developmental prospects and future quality of life—can be announced in such a way that the parents' own perspective is to some degree coimplicated in the clinical assessment.

There are numerous ways, varying in complexity, in which the PDS is used to emphasise congruence and reduce disjuncture between parents' opinions and clinical evaluations, but for present purposes one example will suffice. Extract (2) above continues in the following way:

(5) From Maynard 1991: 468

```
 1→  Dr E:   What do you see? as- his difficulty.
 2→  Mrs C:  Mainly his uhm- the fact that he doesn't understand
 3            everything and also the fact that his speech is
 4            very hard to understand what he's saying, lots of
 5            time
 6   Dr E:   Right.
 7   Dr E:   Do you have any ideas WHY it is? are you- do you?
 8   Mrs C:  No
 9→  Dr E:   Okay I you know I think we BASICALLY in some ways
10            agree with you, insofar as we think that D's MAIN
11            problem, you know DOES involve you know LANGuage,
12→  Mrs C:  Mm hmm
13   Dr E:   You know both you know his- being able to
14            underSTAND, and know what is said to him, and also
15            certainly also to be able to express, you know his
16            uh thoughts
17            (1.0)
18   Dr E:   Um, in general his development ((continues with
              clinical diagnosis))
```

The four arrowed turns here show the basic pattern of the perspective-display series in medical interaction, which structurally speaking is very similar to that described earlier for conversation. Line 1 shows the perspective-display invitation, which is followed in line 2 by a turn in which the parent formulates her son's problems. In this case, the first turn actually mentions the child's 'difficulty' thus providing an indication of precisely what type of perspective is being invited from the parent. However it can also be noted that even when the initial inquiry is couched in more neutral terms, as in extract (4) above ('I just wanted to know from YOU. HOW you see J at this time'), the parent nevertheless orients to it as asking for a 'problem' assessment (which in extract (4) is 'Uhm he can't talk').

Following the parent's perspective display, the doctor produces an agreement token ('Right', line 6), then after a probe for further detail which gets a negative response (lines 7 and 8), embarks on his own perspective which is cast in terms of a basic agreement with what the parent says (lines 9–10) but also exhibits features that mark it as a clinical perspective. First, the doctor uses the term 'we' in phrases such as 'we BASICALLY in some ways agree with you' and ' we think that D's MAIN problem...'. This is a standard feature of clinical discourse, especially in the diagnostic phase, by which doctors speak from the perspective of the medical profession rather than as individuals, invoking institutionally legitimised bodies of knowledge that render what they are saying in terms of professional expertise. Second, the doctor slightly reformulates the parent's description of the child's problem as being to do with 'speech' and describes it as a problem with 'language'. As the following extract also shows, 'language' is the preferred clinical term:

(6) From Maynard 1991: 469
1   Dr E: Wu- whatta you think his PRoblem is
2   Mrs M: Speech
3→   Dr E: Yeah. Yeah his main problem is a- you know a
4   LANguage problem
5→   Mrs M: Yeah language

Here, we similarly find a perspective-display invitation followed by a (very brief) perspective display, which is then agreed with by the doctor before the production of a clinical perspective which differs in its terminology from the parents' statement. Following that, the parent topicalises the clinical perspective (line 4; see also the parent's 'Mm hmm' in line 12 of extract (5)).

This, then, is the basic structural pattern for the PDS in medical interaction:

Perspective-display series in medical interaction
1. Clinician solicits client's perspective
2. Client produces perspective
3. Clinician elaborates on, or reformulates, client's perspective in line with clinical diagnosis
4. Client topicalises clinician's perspective

Although it is structurally similar to the PDS found in conversation, this pattern is fitted to the institutional contingencies of pediatric consultations in a number of ways. First, it overtly situates the parents of young children as valid possessors of knowledge about their child's condition, even if that knowledge may ultimately be shown to differ from the clinical diagnosis yet to be stated. Second, the perspective-display invitation itself frequently mentions the child's 'problem' or 'difficulty'; and even where it does not, it is treated by the parent as requesting an opinion on that topic. Third, the sequence enables potentially upsetting news to be delivered in such a way that the recipient (the parent) is not only consulted as to their view but can find that view coimplicated in the delivery of diagnostic news itself.

Perspective displays in child counselling

Turning now to the child counselling data, we find that perspective-display invitations are frequently produced by counsellors. They are often couched in terms of what the child 'thinks' or 'feels' about a particular issue. For example:

(7)
1   C: Amanda what j'think about goin' t'see yuh dad.

(8)
1   C: Why d'you think they said you couldn't go.

(9)
1   C: Why d'you think, (0.3) mum an' dad said what they said.

(10)
1   C: What does it feel like havin' the houses so far apa:rt.

(11)
1   C: what if you said no to mum.

There are some basic similarities here with the situation just described for pediatric interactions. Perspective-display invitations are produced by the institutional agent (counsellor) rather than the client (child); and the perspective-display invitation itself is designed in the light of specific interactional work involved in the setting. In the above extracts, counsellors' utterances focus on the child's responses, thoughts or feelings in relation to potentially problematic family events. These include seeing a parent in the context of a family separation (extract 7); being told upsetting news by disputing parents (extracts 8 and 9); having parents living separately (extract 10); or potentially 'standing up to' a parent (extract 11). (Later in the chapter these turns are shown again in the sequential contexts in which they were produced.)

In other examples, particular issues are not foregrounded but a more 'generic' inquiry (such as 'How are things at home?') nevertheless results in what can be seen as counselling-relevant news:

(12) C07/00.1:B
1   C: How uh things going?
2   (0.5)
3   P: Fine.
4→   C: What's bin happ'nin[g,
5   (D):   [Fa:h fa::[:h
6→   C: [Down at the ra:nch,

```
 7         (.)
 8 →  P:   Erm:, Well we saw daddy, (0.2) last week an' we saw 'im
 9         the week before.=
10    C:   =What you wen' out with him.
11         (0.3)
12    P:   Um, yeah he came- we::- he s–picked us up, an' we went to
13         his house.
14    C:   He picked y- (0.4) so:, yih da:d came t'pi-=all four of
15         you.
16         (.)
17    D:   Yea[h ( )
18    C:      [But that's the first time since Christmas.
```

Prior to the start of this extract, the children (four siblings) and the counsellor had been engaging in some small talk about the trip to McDonald's the children had been treated to before coming to the session. C's turn in line 1 comes after a pause and seeks to initiate a new line of talk, this time focusing on how 'things' have been 'going'. Perhaps because of its similarity to generic inquiries such as 'How are you?' or 'How's things?', it attracts a standard 'no problem' response: 'Fine' (Jefferson 1980). However, C's next turn exhibits that this was not the kind of response he was seeking by pursuing a perspective, this time specifying, with the colloquial 'Down at the ra:nch', that he is enquiring about things at home. That second attempt, while it similarly does not nominate a particular home-related issue, is followed with an announcement that the children have started to see their father again for 'the first time since Christmas' (at the time of the recording it was July). Thus, while there are an indefinite number of factors that could constitute a perspective on 'things at home', P selects one that is particularly salient in this setting. This is similar to the situation described in extract (4) above, where a clinician's invitation that did not nominate a specific problem nevertheless resulted in a problem-oriented perspective from a parent.

However, this extract does not develop into a perspective-display series since the counsellor elects in subsequent turns to topicalise the child's announcement, rather than producing a perspective of his own on the topic of things 'Down at the ra:nch'. The extract is, in fact, atypical in the data corpus precisely in the way that the child produces a counselling-relevant news announcement in response to a counsellor invitation. As we look at further data extracts, it will become clear that children far more frequently exhibit varying degrees of reluctance to volunteer the kinds of talk about feelings or announcements of counselling-relevant events that counsellors' perspective-display invitations seem to be probing for. Indeed the sequences of talk that such invitations typically engender in the child counselling data result in significant differences from the kinds of patterns discussed above. Those differences reveal more about the kind of therapeutic vision that child counsellors seek to deploy, as well as the extent to which therapeutic objects in this setting are in fact collaboratively produced.

Extract (12) above is taken from a session that involves four siblings: two young brothers ('Greg', 5 and 'Dan', 8) and two older sisters ('Pam', 10 and 'Amanda', 12). As we saw, at least one of them, Pamela, seems keen to tell C about the reappearance of their father on the scene. However, shortly afterwards, C begins to pursue their responses in more depth and other children show markedly less enthusiasm. In the following extract from the same session C directs a perspective-display invitation towards Amanda in the midst of some excitable talk from her younger brother Dan:

```
(13)   C07/00.1:B
 1→  C:    So what- what d'you think,
 2    D:    An' we're ha[vin' this teacher called-
 3→  C:              [Amanda what j'think about goin' t'see yuh
 4          da[d.
 5    D:       [We're havin' this [new teacher called ( )
 6    C:                          [Yer bein' very >quiet='old it< shh!
 7          (.) shush °a minute shush,°
 8          (0.2)
 9→  A:    I don't mi:nd really.
10          (0.9)
11   (D):  ku[hh ((cough))
12→  C:      [Mind really.
13   (D):  kuh hugh
14          (1.2)
15    D:    Mand[y:,
16→  C:        [Mmm do I sense a bit uv, (.) I'm not so su:re.
17→         (1.1)
18    D:    ([       )
19    C:    [Some good bits (.) an' some not suh good bits.
20→         (0.8)
21    D:    Ple:ase can I ha-
22→         (1.6)
23    A:    No jus' the same as Pam really like- [(.) y'get t'miss=
24    D:                                         [Please c'n I have=
25    A:    =[on some-]
26    D:    [a little  ] (Man[dy)
27    A:                     [.h No:.
```

28	C:	[[Yih get t' miss o̲ut on bit[s.
29	A:	[[Yih get t'miss out- [Bu- Da̲n give me back my
30		jui̲[ce.
31	D:	[(([ )
32	C:	[Da̲:n, (0.3) Da̲:n,
33	A:	No̲::wu[h.
34	P:	[Da̲n.

((Talk continues regarding D's purloining of A's drink))

Here, we begin to see some of the features of the perspective-display series as it characteristically occurs in the child counselling data. C invites A's perspective on the topic of 'goin' t'see yuh dad' in lines 1–4. However, after a short pause, A's response is brief and noncommittal: 'I don't mi̲:nd really' (line 9). Following this there is a longer pause of almost a second (line 10) before C produces a partial repeat of A's turn (line 12). That partial repeat notably performs a particular operation on the prior turn, recasting it in different terms by shifting the pattern of emphasis. Whereas A placed the emphasis on 'mind' in 'I don't mi̲:nd really' (line 9), C emphasises 'really' in 'Mind re̲ally' (line 12). The effect of this is to transform the perspective from one of mild indifference to one which potentially manifests scepticism or uncertainty about the topic of 'goin' t'see yuh dad'. In other words, C can be understood here to be proffering a version of A's perspective: an interpretation which she herself may or may not wish to go along with.

However, what follows is another silence during which A declines to expand on her viewpoint (line 14); and (leaving out of account for now Dan's interjacent utterances requesting some of Amanda's drink) C subsequently pursues his own perspective on A's feelings about seeing her father. Lines 16 ('M̲mm do I sense a bi̲t uv, (.) I'm not so su̲:re') and 19 ('Some good bits (.) an' some no̲t suh good bits') seek to do this work in the environment of numerous long pauses (lines 14, 17, 20 and 22) during which this alternative perspective is not topicalised by A.

When Amanda does elect to speak again she begins to produce the pursued expansion on her perspective (lines 23–5); yet it is noticeable that she does not explicitly align with C's proferred version emphasising uncertainty, but instead with her sister Pamela's view (expressed in a previous exchange) that seeing their father merely means that they sometimes miss out on other weekend events. C then shifts position in an attempt to topicalise this view (line 28) but the line of talk is disrupted at that point by Amanda directing her attention towards Dan who, following his earlier unsuccessful requests (see lines 21, 24–6, and A's self-interruptive refusal in line 27), has taken Amanda's drink for himself. Others in the room, including the counsellor, now also turn their attention towards Dan's actions, and the perspective-display series is abandoned at that point.

Thus, although this extract is complex due to the number of children involved in the session, we can see in it a PDS structure which is different in many respects to the structures outlined earlier for conversation and medical interaction. A perspective is invited by the counsellor; but the child gives only a brief and noncommittal view; moreover she seems reluctant subsequently to expand upon it. The counsellor then produces utterances which suggest a slightly different perspective—and one which is noticeably counselling-relevant in that it seeks to foreground supposed doubts in the child's orientation to her visits to the absent father. But that alternative perspective is not topicalised subsequently by the child, and in fact what follows is a shift in the topical focus of the talk.

Further extracts show a very similar pattern. For example, extract (14) comes from early on in a session where the counsellor is trying to explore the child's reaction to having a trip to Disneyland with his father cancelled by his estranged parents who had each blamed the other for the cancellation:

```
(14)   C:23/99.3b:B
   1    C:  So what-what- what d'you think happened=who- who said
   2        you couldn't go.
   3        (0.7)
   4    P:  Both of them.
   5    C:  Bo:th of them,
   6        (2.5)
   7    C:  Are you surprised they said you couldn't go.
   8    P:  Yeah,
   9    C:  You are.
  10    P:  Mm.
  11        (1.0)
  12→   C:  Why d'you think they said you couldn't go.
  13→   P:  Mmm don't know,
  14        (1.2)
  15→   P:  Mm wanna start dra:win'.
  16    C:  Does- do::, (0.2) the fights that mum and dad have, stop
  17        you doing other things.
  18    P:  Yea-a[h.
  19    C:       [What kind've things d'they stop you doing.
  20        (2.4)
  21    P:  Mm-ooh I don't know.
  22    C:  Mm.
  23        (3.8)
  24→   C:  Why d'you think, (1.8) mum an' dad said what they said.
```

```
25         (0.4)
26    P:   Don't know,
27         (4.1)
28 →  C:   Cuz it sounds like they were a bit cross.
29         (0.6)
30    P:   Don't know,
31 →  C:   Who d'you think they're cross with.=
32    P:   =Don't kno[w,
33    C:            [.h O:h I think you do:[:, I think you're=
34    P:                                   [huh huh, .hhh hih=
35    C:   =[playing games with me.
36    P:   =[hih .hhh hih hih
37         (1.6)
38 →  C:   Have I got to try an'- .h will you say don't know all
39         evening.
40         (.)
41    P:   Don't know.
42    C:   Hmm.
```

The perspective-display invitation in line 12 once again receives a brief and noncommittal response from the child (line 13's 'Mmm don't know,' has the audible quality of a kind of 'verbal shrug'). After a pause the child then attempts to shift topic in line 15; C however declines the request to move to the activity of drawing in favour of pursuing information about P's response to the situation regarding his parents and the cancelled trip. Although his questions receive only minimal responses (lines 18 and 21), C nonetheless issues another perspective-display invitation in line 24. We find the same pattern as before: a noncommittal response (line 26) followed by silence (line 27). At that point the counsellor introduces his own perspective, one which, again, brings to the fore a therapeutically relevant interpretation of events: 'Cuz it sounds like they were a bit cross.' There is, however, no subsequent uptake of this perspective by P, despite C's pursuit of it in line 31; and shortly afterwards the topic is abandoned as C introduces a 'game' directed towards attempting to discourage P from responding to all questions with 'Don't know' (for further detail on this particular aspect, see Chapter 6).

The following two extracts exhibit the same basic pattern:

(15) C19/99.1a
```
     ((J is drawing))
     1    C:   Cu- w'z the::re- (.) When- when we spoke, la:st time we
     2         met.
     3         (.)
```

```
 4    J:  Ye:[ah,
 5→   C:      [Is there anything that, (0.2) that you tho:ught about
 6             or that you wanted to talk about today about. (0.9) From
 7             what we talked abo[ut.
 8→   J:                         [N:o. (0.5) Not reall(h)y,[h
 9    C:                                                    [Any- any
10             questions you had from that. Or anything.
11            (1.1)
12    J:  Uh would've a:sked you when we were doin' it.=
13    C:  =A:h kay.
14            (1.6)
15→   C:  C'n y' remember the kind of things we t- did talk about.
16    J:  Yeah.
17            (.)
18→   C:  What- what s:ticks in your mi:nd the most.
19            (.)
20→   J:  (.hh) The magne:ts::, (.) .h a::nd, (.) when I was
21             drawing about .hh how I felt:. The fish.
22    C:  What like when you were (f-)talkin' about bein' caught
23             in, .hh (.) a net. Two nets an' bein' pu[lle  ]d in the=
24    J:                                               [Mm.]
25    C:  =opposite direction, (0.3) That one.
26            (0.9)
27    J:  .h Yeah.
28→   C:  Did i- >Whadabou-=What< I remember about that in
29             particular, .hh was you sayin' that, .mh the worry, (0.3)
30             w:a:s that .hh you had one net pullin:g, (.) one fishing
31             net pullin:g, in one direction, (0.2) another fishing net
32             pulling from the other direction, .hh an' then .hh an'
33             then you sayin' that y- your worry, .h was that you this
34             little fish in the middle,
35    J:  Mm,
36    C:  Suddenly both nets would s:nap an' split in ha:lf, (.)
37             an' you would kind of sink tuh the bottom uthe sea: an'
38             be left all alo:ne.
39→          (1.9)
40    C:  I remember that.
41→          (2.8) ((J finishes her drawing))
42→   J:  What d'you think.=
```

```
43→  C:  =That sounded >really important.< .hh Yeah I like the
44        dog. (0.8) 'As 'e gotta na:me. (0.5) Is it a suh-=I'm
45        sayin' he is it a he or is it a she.
46        (0.2)
47   J:  He::It's:: a::, (0.2) he.
```

A perspective-display invitation couched in neutral terms (beginning in line 5) receives a noncommittal response and is then pursued (lines 15 and 18). In this instance, the child does cooperate slightly more than in the two previous extracts, offering a view on what aspects of her drawing in the prior session 'stick in her mind the most' (lines 20–1). C seeks to topicalise those aspects of the drawing in his next turn, but following a pause (line 26) J produces no further talk beyond a confirmation. C then moves to produce a perspective of his own on the drawing, foregrounding potential therapeutic matters such as the child's fear that 'Suddenly both nets would s:nap an' split in ha:lf, (.) an' you would kind of sink tuh the bottom uthe sea: an' be left all alo:ne.' This perspective is not topicalised by J (note the pauses in lines 39 and 41), and she subsequently initiates a change in topic by asking C what he thinks of the new drawing she has just finished.

In (16), the child (Peter) has been in the process of producing a drawing depicting the two separate houses that his mother and his father now live in:

```
(16)  C:23/99.3b:B
      ((P is drawing))
      1    C:  What 'ave you written there.
      2         (0.8)
      3    P:  They're numbers tuh show how-wu- [s:how-
      4    C:                                   [To show how far away it
      5         is.
      6         (6.6)
      7→   C:  What does it feel like havin' the houses so far apa:rt.
      8         (1.9)
      9→   P:  Don't know,
      10→  C:  Does it feel like this picture?
      11        (1.2)
      12→  C:  (It feels) that picture looks, (0.9) a bit sad.
      13→       (2.2)
      14   C:  Does this face ever get happy,
      15→       (3.0)
      16   C:  What makes that face happy.=
      17   P:  =°(Don't know.)°
```

Again, we find the same components. C produces a perspective-display invitation (line 7) which once more focuses on the child's 'feelings'; this is followed by a pause and a noncommittal response (line 9). C pursues a feelings-based perspective in line 10, trying to encourage P to conceive of his feelings in terms of the drawing he has made. Following the lack of a response at line 11, C proffers his own interpretation of the feelings depicted in the drawing ('that picture looks… a bit sad'). Again, however, in subsequent turns that perspective is not topicalised by the child.

In summary, the pattern is that a perspective is invited by the counsellor to which the child responds only briefly or noncommitally. The counsellor then pursues a perspective but receives either no response or a similarly noncommittal one from the child. The counsellor then volunteers a perspective of his own which seeks to foreground therapeutically relevant matters. The child declines to topicalise that perspective and the series is abandoned by means of a shift in topic or activity. We can thus represent the basic structural form of the perspective-display series in the child counselling data as follows:

Perspective-display series in child counselling
1. Counsellor solicits child's perspective
2. Child produces noncommittal response or declines to respond
3. Counsellor pursues a perspective
4. Child declines or produces brief/noncommittal response
5. Counsellor produces own perspective
6. Child declines uptake

Counselling perspectives and therapeutic vision

Maynard (1991: 460) speculates 'that the circuitous way in which the PDS allows arrival at a third-turn "report" is an inherently cautious maneouvre that makes the series particularly adaptable to environments of professional-lay interaction, conversations among unacquainted parties, and so on.' It is also, as Maynard (1991) showed, suitable for environments in which bad news or an upsetting diagnosis is about to be delivered. We might therefore imagine that the strategy would be suited to environments in which delicate topics are brought into play; and as indicated at the start of this chapter, child counselling in situations of parental separation is one such setting.

However, it seems that the PDS does not function particularly well in child counselling: not, at least, in the sense it operates in the pediatric consultations studied by Maynard (1991) where the series can enable the client (parent) to find their own viewpoint coimplicated in the clinical diagnosis. It is possible that child counsellors seek their clients' (children's) perspectives for similar reasons; namely so that the child's viewpoint can be built into the therapeutic work of the counselling session. Counsellors are trained to avoid 'leading' their clients, and child counsellors especially are also encouraged to situate the child's own 'story' at the centre of their work (Geldard and Geldard 1997). Therefore, using a variant of the perspective-display series might seem a good interactional strategy. But the key point about the PDS is that the 'third turn report' (produced by the series initiator) is heavily reliant on a successful second turn perspective to which it can be shown to be responsive. It is the lack of such a second turn perspective—that is, one oriented towards potentially counselling-relevant matters—from the children in the above extracts that leads to the PDS in child counselling taking the particular shape it does.

The differences between the invitation and display of perspectives in child counselling, in conversation and in pediatric consultations can thus be traced to two factors. First, the interactional work that the initiator of the series is seeking to do; and second, the degree of cooperation accorded to that unfolding enterprise by the interlocutor. In conversation, it may simply be that the first speaker is seeking to explore the types of views held or the level of knowledge possessed by a second in relation to some mutually relevant topic. As Maynard (1991) suggests, the cautiousness of the strategy makes it suited to conversations between relatively unacquainted parties because it provides a sequential environment in which, if necessary, congruence between opinions can be maximised and conflict minimised or avoided altogether. For the PDS to succeed, therefore, the second speaker needs to collaborate not only in providing their own perspective, but in subsequently topicalising the first speaker's perspective in the fourth move of the sequence:

Perspective-display series in conversation
1. A solicits B's perspective
2. B produces perspective
3. A produces own perspective, taking account of B's
4. B topicalises A's perspective

In medical (pediatric) consultations, a different kind of interactional work is involved but the same conditions hold. The clinician may not be inviting the client's perspective in any 'naïve' way in the course of a mutual exploration of viewpoints, but seeking to create an environment in which a potentially upsetting diagnosis can be introduced more 'softly' than if it were just straightforwardly announced. But again, such a strategy depends on the client not only acquiescing in providing a perspective but also topicalising the clinical perspective:

Perspective-display series in medical interaction

1. Clinician solicits client's perspective
2. Client produces perspective
3. Clinician elaborates on, or reformulates, client's perspective in line with clinical diagnosis
4. Client topicalises clinician's perspective

In child counselling, although it often appears as if the counsellor is simply seeking to explore viewpoints with the child in a sort of conversational mutual exchange (recall the remarks in Chapter 2 on the quasi-conversational nature of the discourse), what happens in subsequent turns indicates that there is an insitutional agenda at work here in which children's perspectives are ideally related to feelings, or to other matters that can be given a counselling-relevance. In fact, that agenda is often built into the design of counsellors' perspective-display invitations in the first place, which as remarked above tend to ask about 'What [X] feels like' or 'What the child thinks about [Y]' (where [X] and [Y] are matters related to the family situation).

It is not possible to say whether or not children possess any awareness or understanding of such an institutional agenda at the time counsellors' utterances are produced. What does seem clear is that their responses exhibit varying degrees of reluctance to engage with such feelings-related topics. Even in the few cases where children are more forthcoming in producing perspectives, talk about feelings, fears and concerns is topicalised more extensively by counsellors than by children. For example, in extract (15) J mentions 'how I felt:' in her turn following a perspective-display invitation, the past tense indicating that she is now reporting on what she remembers about the drawing she did in the previous session:

```
(15)   (Detail)
 15    C:   C'n y' remember the kind of things we t- did talk about.
 16    J:   Yeah.
 17         (.)
 18    C:   What- what s:ticks in your mi:nd the most.
 19         (.)
 20→   J:   (.hh) The magne:ts::, (.) .h a::nd, (.) when I was
 21→        drawing about .hh how I felt:. The fish.
```

The counsellor in this case subsequently produces his own perspective on this which foregrounds the child's fears:

(15) (Detail)
```
    28 → C:   Did i- >Whadabou-=What< I remember about that in
    29        particular, .hh was you sayin' that, .mh the worry, (0.3)
    30        w:a:s that .hh you had one net pullin:g, (.) one fishing
    31        net pullin:g, in one direction, (0.2) another fishing net
    32        pulling from the other direction, .hh an' then .hh an'
    33        then you sayin' that y- your worry, .h was that you this
    34        little fish in the middle,
    35   J:   Mm,
    36   C:   Suddenly both nets would s:nap an' split in ha:lf, (.)
    37        an' you would kind of sink tuh the bottom uthe sea: an'
    38        be left all alo:ne.
```

Note how this turn begins with the phrase 'What I remember about that in particular', emphasising that what follows is C's own recollection which, of course, may or may not differ from that of the child. Whereas J had merely mentioned 'how I felt:', C's turn explicitly mentions 'the worry' (line 29) and 'your worry' (line 33): a worry that is presented using the graphic image of 'sink[ing] tuh the bottom uthe sea: an' be[ing] left all alo:ne'. Nevertheless, having previously cooperated by producing a perspective (albeit briefly), the child declines to take this topic up in further talk (in spite of C's later remark that 'That sounded really important').

In the majority of cases, children exhibit far more reluctance to deliver a perspective, with the result that counsellors end up volunteering counselling-relevant perspectives of their own; although this often follows some pursuit of a child's perspective. As we have seen, a key difference again is that the child declines to topicalise the counsellor's perspective, frequently by means of an attempt to change the topic.

There is thus far less mutual collaboration in the PDS in child counselling than we find in either of the other two types of interaction. Hence, although counsellors' attempts to elicit children's perspectives may be motivated by a desire to avoid leading the child and to orient the session around 'the child's story', the sequential environment that emerges places them in a position of proffering a perspective that is not overtly based on the child's story but on the counsellor's interpretation, which itself tends to index key counselling concerns or—as I go on to discuss in the next chapter—tropes.

Conclusion

This chapter has analysed one of the means by which child counsellors can be said to exercise therapeutic vision: the professional work of seeing in events, actions or utterances phenomena that can be worked up into 'therapeutic objects'. I began by indicating some of the ways in which the child counselling session, although set up and oriented to by counsellors themselves as 'the child's space' to talk about family problems without the pressure of their parents' presence, in fact may be an inauspicious environment for such talk. Key factors are the opacity of frame in terms of the general goals of the counselling session, and the overarching presence of delicate topics, namely the imminent or ongoing break-up of the child's family unit. While children tend to avoid detailed discussion of feelings of anger, guilt or sadness, or concerns and fears about the future, and so on, counsellors nevertheless orient towards the potential existence of such feelings or concerns. They therefore seek to open up spaces in which children may feel disposed to producing such talk.

The perspective-display series is one means by which this is done. Use of the PDS can be said to be responsive to two partially conflicting professional imperatives under which counsellors operate. First, their professional (therapeutic) vision, which encourages them to try and topicalise 'difficult' issues in order to help the child to appreciate alternative perspectives that may help them to understand what is going on in their lives. Second, the basic training imperative to act as a facilitator or conduit and avoid taking up too 'active' a role in the production of talk (an issue I return to in Chapter 5).

The conflicting nature of these imperatives becomes observable in the very organisation of the PDS as it occurs in the data discussed above. Faced with a situation in which children avoid producing the kinds of perspectives counsellors are seeking, counsellors resort to producing perspectives themselves—or at least, to putting such perspectives forward so that the child may accept or decline them. As it turns out, children seem ultimately to decline the whole line of talk involved in the PDS. The PDS is thus one interactional environment in which we can observe the relevance of 'therapeutic vision' and the ways that children seek to deal with counsellors' exercise of it—that is, fairly consistently, to resist or evade it.

CHAPTER 5

Active listening and the formulation of concerns

In this chapter I address further aspects of how counselling-relevant matters are topicalised in the course of interaction between counsellors and children.[1] The focus turns towards a practice that is often referred to as a key skill for counsellors and therapists: not just those involved with children, but in a wide variety of practice settings. In textbooks on counselling techniques, such a skill is referred to as 'active listening'.

Like many counselling techniques, certain elements of active listening are in fact very similar to procedures involved in the production of ordinary conversation. Conversation analysts have noted that in order to manage successful turn-taking in conversation, participants need to be not simply hearing, but actively listening to the talk of their interlocutor(s) (Sacks, Schegloff and Jefferson 1974). As we know from the phenomenon of supermarket muzak, among other things, one can be 'hearing' a sound without actually 'listening' to it. The difference is that in listening, within conversation, one is inevitably engaged in interpreting, making sense of, and usually responding to an utterance. By the same token, participants are involved in a process by which their own next utterance is to be oriented to for how it proposes an understanding of the co-participant's prior utterance.

In child counselling, this practice comes to be bound up with the constitution of the counselling framework itself, in its activity of monitoring the child's talk for possible ways into a therapeutic interpretation or intervention. The counsellor's active listening in relation to even minor aspects of the child's talk plays a key role in the success of the session's work: the work of inciting the child to communicate about his or her experiences. In the following analysis I focus on one particular active listening practice by means of which counsellors monitor, interpret and construct the meaning of children's utterances in order to bring into play possible 'concerns' about family relationships—a process that in general can be described as the elicitation of feelings-talk.

---

1. An earlier version of this chapter appeared as 'Active listening: Formulations and the elicitation of feelings-talk in child counselling', *Research on Language and Social Interaction*, 38: 303–29 (2005).

Active listening in child counselling

'Active listening' is often referred to as one of the key skills of counselling; particularly, though not only, child counselling. For example, in their practical introduction to child counselling techniques, Geldard and Geldard (1997: 53) state that:

> Counselling skills need to be relevant for the various stages of the therapeutic process. Generally this therapeutic process will span a series of sessions during which the counsellor will need to perform a number of different counselling functions:
>
> - joining with the child;
> - observation of the child;
> - **active listening**;
> - awareness raising and the resolution of issues to facilitate change;
> - dealing with the child's beliefs
> - actively facilitating change;
> - termination of counselling.

Similarly, Sharpe and Cowie (1998: 81) state that:

> Counselling-based approaches [to helping children] vary widely in emphasis, encompassing issues like bullying, loneliness, adjusting to a new school, and dealing with separation and loss. But there are some common elements in these ... including ... basic skills of **active listening**, empathy, problem solving and supportiveness.

But what is 'active listening?' In general, the term is intended to convey a sense that counsellors are 'able to help the child to tell her story and to identify troubling issues. In doing this the child must know that we are paying attention and valuing the information that we are receiving' (Geldard and Geldard 1997: 57). Geldard and Geldard (1997: 57–64) expand on this by discussing practical techniques that child counsellors may use to engage in active listening. These include 'reflecting' and 'summarizing'. In 'reflecting', the counsellor is enjoined to 'pick out the most important content details of what the child has said and re-express them in a clearer way' (Geldard and Geldard 1997: 59). In 'summarizing', the counsellor 'draws together the main points in the content, and also takes into account the feelings which the child has described' (op. cit.: 63). Sharpe and Cowie (1998: 85) refer to similar terms but with less specificity: '[counselling] skills include active, empathic listening, summarising and reflecting back the accounts and narratives of ... "clients", allowing space and time for the expression of emotions, learning not to offer advice too early, and collaborating ... to develop a problem-solving stance'.

In other words, active listening seeks to advance the goals of counselling and the therapeutic process by, first, providing an interactional context in which the child feels comfortable and trusting enough to 'tell their story'. Second, in facilitating that telling, it enables the counsellor to identify, draw out, and make interactionally available 'feelings' expressed in the course of the story.

This, however, is an ideal model, and it is not immediately clear from either Geldard and Geldard's (1997) or Sharpe and Cowie's (1998) accounts how that model maps onto the reality of child counselling. One possible consequence is that practising child counsellors may be encouraged to evaluate their own real-world sessions against the ideal model and, perhaps, find them wanting. In fact, when we observe the techniques used by counsellors in the real-time unfolding of their interactions with children, we see that such ideal models map only loosely at best onto the therapeutic interchange. The relevance of analyses such as this one, therefore, is that conversation analysis can reveal the practical skills that counsellors use—often regardless of models recommended by their training—to accomplish outcomes amidst the contingencies of turn by turn talk-in-interaction (see also Peräkylä 1995; Silverman 1996).

This is significant because, as suggested by the above quoted remarks on 'reflecting' and 'summarising', what counsellors are told about the nuts and bolts of how to do active listening tends to be highly generalised, and correspondingly vague. This may be because the unavoidable context-sensitivity of turns at talk means that precisely how a speaker could go about summarising or drawing together feelings-relevant points in a prior utterance is essentially unspecifiable in advance, except by the recommendation of formulaic utterances such as 'What I hear you saying is . . .' which in themselves may not always be contextually appropriate.[2] Geldard and Geldard (1997: 59–62) do provide a range of examples of 'reflecting'-type utterances, but it is not made clear whether their examples are taken from actual child counselling talk or are invented. The following example suggests that it is likely that they are, in fact, invented, and hence formulaic:

> Child statement: Every time I ask Mum if I can go to Aunty Karen's she says 'No'. Kelly's going this weekend and it was my turn.
> Possible counsellor responses: *You're disappointed*, or *You sound angry*. [The correct response would depend on the context and on non-verbal cues.]   (Geldard and Geldard 1997: 61)

Associated with these points is the model of the counsellor that underpins such descriptions of active listening as those quoted above. In these descriptions, it is as if the counsellor's role is to act as a conduit, a largely neutral presence 'drawing together' and 're-expressing' or clarifying the 'feelings' described by the child. In other words, the child's talk is held to contain authentic expressions of feelings

---

2. As Puchta and Potter (1999) found in their study of the relationship between training manuals and actual practice in conducting focus groups, generic advice on 'best practice' (such as 'ask clear, simple questions') is undermined when the talk is situated within the contingencies of interaction (where it may be far more appropriate, even necessary, to ask fairly elaborated questions). See also Suchman and Jordan (1990) for a discussion of related issues in the context of standardised interviews for social scientists, market researchers and others.

which, while they may not be immediately apparent, can be revealed through the practices of reflecting and summarizing.

However, what becomes clear when we look at the practical accomplishment of active listening in naturally-occuring child counselling dialogues is that the technique is much more 'constructive' or 'directive' than it is simply 'active'; indeed it is less a matter of 'listening' per se, and more a matter of 'listening for a way to formulate what is said as therapeutically relevant'. Given the general reluctance of children to topicalise their concerns in this setting, counsellors can be seen to orient to children's talk as if it contains signs, or indices, of unarticulated concerns. Such concerns, which the policy of active listening may encourage counsellors to feel are nonetheless present, thus have to be constructed as ratifiable artefacts in the public domain of discourse.

In the following analysis, active listening is approached as part of the practical, contingent and interactionally skilful work of counsellors and children as cultural members, rather than the abstract recommendations of handbooks and training manuals. In a nutshell, active listening is seen as a term of therapeutic art that needs to be explicated through fine-grained examination of actual practice. The focus is on counsellors' production of 'formulations' of children's talk and the subsequent responses to those formulations: whether cooperative or, in a small proportion of cases, seemingly resistive.

Formulations and the work of child counselling

As noted in Chapter 2, textbooks on child counselling frequently instruct the counsellor to avoid asking questions. As Geldard and Geldard (1997: 11) put it, 'There is a danger in asking too many questions, because the child may fear being asked to disclose information which is private and/or too scary to share.' Nevertheless, the chapters so far illustrate that counsellors routinely initiate question-answer sequences with children. One reason for this may be the very reluctance of children themselves to topicalise family-related concerns. The asking of questions allows counsellors to exert some control over the topical direction of the session. But more than that, certain categories of question, or question-types, enable counsellors to draw out of the child talk about feelings or other counselling-relevant matters. One type of question-answer sequence that is of interest in this respect involves the counsellor following up the child's answer with a formulation.

Formulation is a conversational practice (see Garfinkel and Sacks 1970; Heritage and Watson 1979; Heritage 1985) which Heritage (1985: 100) describes as 'summarizing, glossing, or developing the gist of an informant's earlier statements'. He goes on to suggest that formulation is 'relatively rare in conversation', but regularly occurs in certain forms of institutional interaction, where it is it is 'most commonly undertaken by questioners' (Heritage 1985: 100). In his study of formulations in broadcast news interviews, Heritage (1985) found that the practice could be used both in a relatively benign, summarizing role ('cooperative recyclings'), and also as a means by which the questioner seeks to evaluate or criticise the respondent's remarks ('inferentially elaborative probes').

Heritage proposes that formulations are neutral in the sense that they avoid commenting on or making assessments of the content of a prior turn. However, as the 'inferentially elaborative probe' category suggests, formulations can in fact 'make something more of [a topic] than was originally presented in the ... prior turn' (Heritage 1985: 101). Thus, formulations are not always entirely neutral. What they do is to act as candidate re-presentations of what an interlocutor can be taken as having said, or meant. Such candidate re-presentations are selective, in that they focus on a particular element of the prior talk and preserve that element as the topic for further talk. They can also be driven by an underlying agenda on their producer's part, which in turn can be cooperative, uncooperative or openly argumentative. And they open a sequential slot in which the interlocutor may, in the next turn, accept, reject or otherwise respond to the formulation. But whatever the response, the formulation reveals its producer not as a neutral conduit but an active interpreter of the preceding talk.[3]

Formulations occur frequently in the child counselling data, and they are invariably produced by counsellors, not by children. This is consistent with Heritage's (1985) observation that formulations in institutional forms of talk tend to get produced by speakers occupying professional or institutionally-representative roles (e.g. doctors, therapists, interviewers and so on)—in other words, those whose typical turn-taking role tends to be that of questioner (Drew and Heritage 1992).

In the data analysed below, the focus is on those occasions when a counsellor follows up a question-answer sequence with a formulation. Formulations may occasion a response from the recipient in the next turn, in which the interpretation offered of their prior talk may be agreed or disagreed with. However, such response turns do not always occur (see, for instance, extract 1 below). Thus, for the sake of convenience I will refer to this simply as a Question-Answer-Formulation (QAF) sequence—even though, as we will see below, further talk occasioned by counsellors' formulations also plays a major part in the elicitation of feelings-talk. In

---

[3]. In the counselling and psychotherapy literature, such a practice is often referred to as 'reformulation'. Given these comments about the non-neutral status of inferentially elaborative probe-type formulations, it might be that '*re*formulation' is in fact a more accurate term. However, due to the prevalence of the term 'formulation' in the conversation analytic literature, I will continue to use that term, while bearing in mind that the practice typically involves the production of non-neutral, candidate re-presentations of a prior stretch of talk.

the following examples, as in other work on formulations, the formulation itself is often marked out by the use of a prefatory item, 'So', in turn-initial position (as in 'So you're saying that...' or 'So what that means is...'). But not all turns beginning with the particle 'so' in the following data are in fact formulations. For this reason lettered arrows have been used to mark out analytically relevant sequences. The relevant question is marked by an arrow (Q), the child's answer by arrow (A), and the formulation by arrow (F).

Extract (1) is taken from a session involving two young brothers and two older sisters. Early on in the session, the children have informed the counsellor that they have recently seen their father for the first time in months, and have visited at his home:

```
(1)  C07/00.1:B
     1  Q→  C:    So: how many times ev y'seen 'im since w'last met.
     2  A→  (D):  °°Two°°=
     3  A→  (P):  =°°Two°°
     4  F→  C:    Twi:ce. Is it- So tw[o Sundays in a row.
     5      (P):               [°Yeh°
     6            (1.0)
     7      C:    An' er y' gonna see 'im this Sunday.
     8            (.)
     9      D:    Ah think [so,
    10      P:             [Probally.
    11            (0.8)
    12      P:    Yah.
    13            (0.5)
    14      C:    So::, (1.8) What bits o' that do y' like an' what bits
    15            o' that don't y' like.
    16            (2.0)
    17      P:    Erm, (0.4) the on'y bit I don't like is that cuz we 'ave
    18            t'go- (.) cuz we go ev'ry Sunday sometimes we miss out on
    19            doing things,
```

In line 1, the counsellor begins by asking how often the children's visits have taken place. Two of the children offer the same response in lines 2 and 3, and at the start of line 4 the counsellor marks the newsworthiness of this response: 'Twi:ce.' He then appears to embark on the production of a next question ('Is it-') before cutting off and producing a formulation which foregrounds a particular aspect of the news that there have been two visits since the last meeting. With this formulation, 'So two Sundays in a row', the counsellor marks out something about the frequency of these visits. That is, there have not just been two visits, but two visits on consecutive Sundays. In previous sessions, a key topic has been the lack of contact the children have with their father. The counsellor's formulation begins to orient to the possibility that, not only has there now been a contact visit, but there is potentially a regular series of visits underway. There is no verbal response to this formulation in the one second silence at line 6 (the 'Yeh' in line 5 is produced in overlap with C's formulation and seems designed as a confirmation of the preceding 'Twi:ce'). C nevertheless pursues the newsworthiness marked out in his formulation in his next utterance (line 7), where he asks if the visits are likely to continue this week. Indeed, the possibility that there has been the initiation of a weekly visiting routine is made explicit in P's turn at line 18 ('cuz we go ev'ry Sunday').

Three main points should be noted about this extract. First, a 'so'-prefaced formulation is used to mark out as newsworthy something in the children's responses to the counsellor's question; but more than that, precisely what it is that is newsworthy about that something (the initiation of weekly visits) is drawn out as the sequence of talk unfolds following the formulation. Second, the marked news is highly counselling-relevant. In this setting, information regarding frequency of contact between children and absent parents is especially salient—the more so when the noteworthy information concerns a change in those arrangements. Third, the counsellor subsequently seeks to relate that news back to the children's feelings about events, when in lines 14–15 he asks, 'What bits o' that do y' like an' what bits o' that don't y' like.' It is in the context of this follow-up question that one of the children places the 'weekliness' of the visits on record.

In the next extract, two 'so'-prefaced formulations are used in the process of foregrounding another counselling-relevant piece of information. This time the issue under discussion has associations with imagery frequently deployed in materials aimed at helping children to 'deal with' the experience of parental separation, particularly their responses to the occurrence of arguments between parents, which are depicted as involving increased levels of shouting:[4]

```
(2)   C19/99.1:A
Q→  1  C:   How does your mum get your dad to hear what she wants to
      2       say.
A→  3  J:   Oh she shouts:.
Q2→ 4  C:   Does your dad hea[r her.
```

---

4. During observational work in the child counselling practice where the data were collected, I noted a number of story books, picture books and so on distributed around the waiting room and reception area, places where children and their parents would routinely sit whilst waiting for their appointed session time. These books seemed intended to make available to children and possibly parents too a range of 'positive images' around parental separation, rows, violence, blameworthiness and other relevant issues.

A→	5	J:	[She shout really lou̲dly cuz she:'s a
	6		te̲acher and she shouts sort uv .hh she̲'s got thisuh
	7		re̲ally lou[d voice ((squeals))
	8	C:	[.h A:̲hh.
F→	9	C:	So she's good at sort of shou[ting] like, like she's=
	10	J:	[Yeh.]
	11	C:	=be[ing a teacher.
	12	J:	[But she do̲esn- she doesn't do it in such a high
	13		pitched voice. .hh If I did it the bu̲ilding would
	14		probably blow up.
	15		(0.8)
	16	C:	Wha̲t cuz you've got a high pitched voice.
	17		(.)
	18	J:	N[o̲:. Because-]
	19	C:	[O:r just like yo]ur mum.
	20	J:	Because it's:: really lo̲ud.
	21		(0.3)
	22	C:	And your da̲d's le̲arning to be a teacher.
	23	J:	Mmm.
	24	C:	So is he le̲arnin:g to shout [loud too.
	25	J:	[No̲ h(h)e d(h)oesn't
	26		shout.
	27		(.)
Q→	28	C:	Is 'e gunna le̲arn to shout d'y' think like o̲ther
	29		teachers. (.) Or d'you think he'll always no̲t shout.
A→	30	J:	I don't think he wi̲ll shout.
F→	31	C:	So he'll be a kind of teacher that do̲esn't shout.
	32		(2.3)
	33	J:	He do̲esn't like telling them o̲ff.
	34		(0.5)
	35	C:	A:̲:h.
	36		(1.8)
	37	C:	Does 'e shout at yo̲u.
	38		(0.2)
	39	J:	N:::o̲t mu̲::ch,

The first formulation here comes in the context of a discussion about how J perceives differences between her mother who, according to J, 'shout(s) really lou̲dly cuz she's a te̲acher' (lines 5–6), and her more quietly spoken father. J's association between the category 'teachers' and the activity 'shouting' is produced in the course of her answer to C's question in lines 1–2, inquiring about how the mother gets the father 'to hear what she wants to say'. The association is picked up and formulated by the counsellor in lines 9–11. We might notice here a slight shift from the child's description of her mother shouting 'cuz she's a teacher' (line 6), to the counsellor's formulation in which the mother is described as shouting 'like she's being a teacher' (lines 10–11). In this shift, C's formulation foregrounds the fact that the shouting is taking place not in the school, where the mother may be acting straightforwardly as a teacher, but in the home, where she is characterised as acting as if she is being a teacher.

The teaching/shouting association is brought into play by the counsellor again in line 24, where he suggests that learning to be a teacher might lead to the father 'learnin:g to shout'. In line 25, notably, J declines to extend the association to her father, focusing instead on his purported trait as someone who 'd(h)oesn't shout' (significantly, she does not use the future tense, as in 'he won't shout', but the present tense, in her categorical assertion 'he doesn't shout').

At this point, then, to use Sacks's (1972) terms, C is orienting to shouting as a 'category-bound activity' for members of the category teachers, a category-boundedness which J herself had introduced in relation to her mother. However, in relation to her father, J seeks to establish a separation between the category-boundedness of this activity and his actual practice as a category member. In the three turns that follow we find a QAF sequence in which this ambivalence is pursued by the counsellor. His question in line 28 both reiterates the earlier question in line 24, and yet allows for the possibility that the father's 'natural' propensity for non-shouting behaviour may exempt him from the category-boundedness of shouting. J's response in line 30 takes up the latter possibility; and in line 31, C's 'so'-prefaced formulation ('So he'll be a kind of teacher that doesn't shout') foregrounds the breakdown of the category-boundedness between teachers and shouting.

Again, then, 'so'-prefaced formulations are used in the course of topicalising an issue with particular salience in the child counselling setting: differences in behaviour—especially aggressive behaviours such as shouting—between a child's parents. In quite a subtle way, C's pursuit of the strength of the bond between 'being a teacher' and 'shouting' is complicit in the child's differential construction of her parents' personalities, with the father, at this stage in the process, being seen in a considerably more positive light than the mother. A final point to note is the way in which, following the second formulation, the counsellor once again indexes the father's lack of shouting directly back to the child in line 37 ('Does 'e shout at you.').

Extract (3) offers another example of a formulation being used to pick up on and foreground the key issue of differences between parental behaviour and practices:

```
    (3)  C19/99.1:A
Q→ 1        C: .hh (.) .h An' d- do you normally decide what's gunna
    2           happen then.
A→ 3        J:  Normally with my dad but with my mum if I did it, .h I'd
    4           be in s:erious troub[le.
F→ 5        C:                    [A::h. So it's a bit different with
    6           mum than it is with da[d.
    7        J:                       [It's really hard because my dad
    8           tells me t'do one thing and my mum tells me tuh do the
    9           other
```

The counsellor's question in line 1 picks up on previous talk (not shown) to ask about the extent to which the child gets the opportunity to decide about activities undertaken with each of her parents. J's answer provides a number of potential avenues for further talk: for instance, the counsellor could pursue the indication that J has the freedom 'normally' to make decisions when with her father (line 3); or he could follow up on the child's feelings about her mother in light of the reference to 's:erious trouble' (line 4). However, the counsellor elects to formulate J's turn in lines 3–4 in terms of the statement 'it's a bit different with mum than it is with dad' (lines 5–6). More explicitly than in extract (2), this formulation picks up on imagery that is common in storybooks and other literature aimed at children in parental separation, and usually to be found and used as resources in child counselling practices, which depicts estranged parents as frequently contradicting one another, leading to confusion and distress for their children. This can be described as the 'conflicting messages' trope.

Two further points are worth making about this example. First, notice that the counsellor prefaces the formulation with a newsmarker: 'A::h.' (line 5). Newsmarkers are turn-initial items by means of which the recipient of a prior turn can indicate that what was said constitutes either new information for them, or is something of particular noteworthiness (Heritage 1984). The counsellor's utterance is thus produced not simply as a formulation of the child's prior turn, but as a formulation which exhibits that, whether the child knows it or not, something potentially highly significant has just been said. I return to this use of newsmarkers by counsellors in the following section.

Second, notice that the child herself adopts the 'conflicting messages' trope in her next turn (lines 7–9). Indeed, as we see by means of the following extension of extract (3), there ensues an extended sequence of talk in this vein where the child's descriptions in particular are remarkable for their closeness of fit with the kind of imagery provided in 'help' manuals for children in parental separation:

(4) (continuation of Extract 3)
```
        7    J:                    [It's really hard because my dad
        8         tells me t'do one thing and my mum tells me tuh do the
        9         other=.hh=an' it feels a bit like I showed you last week,
       10         .hh with my da:d saying do this and wi' mum saying do
       11         this an' I don't know what t' do:.
       12         (0.7)
F→     13    C:   So y- y- you get told t'do two different things [at  ]the=
       14    J:                                                   [Yeh]
       15    C:   =same ti:me.
       16    J:   An' I don't know what t'do an' then I get in trouble with
       17         my mum an' get in trouble with my dad .hh an' I say well
       18         which one am I meant to do an' they say my one an' I'm
       19         like .hh well you're both saying my one an' they say well
       20         do my one 'n they've both s*aid *it. .hhh
```

The counsellor, in lines 13–15, responds to J's further talk with a second formulation (again prefaced by 'So' but this time lacking the newsmarker) which once again emphasises the conflicting messages trope: the child gets 'told t'do two different things at the same ti:me.'. The child in turn assents to that formulation (line 14) before proceeding, in lines 16–20, to elaborate still further on the topic.

In terms of understanding in detail the work counsellors do to draw out concerns, therefore, formulations are significant on a number of levels. First, like formulations observed in other settings (Heritage and Watson 1979; Heritage 1985), they operate to foreground specific aspects of the child-client's responses to the counsellor's questions. That is, they act as candidate re-presentations of the prior talk which select, and thereby focus on a particular element of that prior talk, seeking to preserve that element as the topic for further talk. More than that, however, such candidate re-presentations are of a particular type. In each of these extracts, the formulations 'home in' on what can be described as 'counselling-relevant' factors: those which potentially assist in topicalising therapeutic matters. These include frequency of parental contact (extract 1); different parental propensities to shout (extract 2); and the provision by parents of conflicting messages, or 'being told to do two things at the same time' (extracts 3 and 4). Third, we have seen that formulations tend to occasion further stretches of related talk, not just in the child's response to the formulating turn itself, but in the way that counsellors may further develop counselling-relevant matters in relation to the child's experience: by asking how they feel about such matters or whether the matter affects them. Thus, the formulation of counselling-relevant matters generally seems to involve the counsellor bringing into play events in the child's 'private' or intrapersonal sphere (feelings, emotions, experiences) and translating them into the 'public' or interpersonal sphere of talk-in-interaction.

Unfolding therapeutic matters

This process of translation between the intra- and interpersonal domains is often bound up with more extended sequences of talk through which therapeutically relevant matters are revealed or made interactionally available. This is shown particularly clearly in the following extract. Here, the ultimate formulation of a segment of feelings-talk is presented as the climax to a set of 'discoveries' which the counsellor makes—and makes available to the child through marking them as such—on the basis of information provided in the child's talk. Note, in this respect, the counsellor's frequent use of the newsmarker 'Ah' (lines 1, 9, 20, 25, 31 and 48).

```
(5)   C19/99.1:A
 1      C:  A::h 'kay so if you did what your da:d (.)
 2          a::sked you or suggested, li[ke  ] go an' play on the=
 3      J:                              [Yeh]
 4      C:  =computer, (0.5) would that happen would your mum an' dad
 5          have an argument about it.
 6      J:  Well they- the:y wouldn't me an' my mum would an' me an'
 7          my dad would. .hh An' my mum an' dad would tell each
 8          other off but they wouldn't argue.
 9      C:  A::h. (.) Is that, different do [they-
10      J:                                  [An' my mum would smack
11          me an' send me up t' bed. [Even-
12      C:                            [Su- What even though she's
13          cross with da:d.
14          (.)
15      J:  [[Yeh.
16      C:  [[She'd smack you?
17          (0.2)
18      J:  Yeah.
19          (0.5)
20      C:  A:h.=But she's cross with dad.
21      J:  Yeh I know.
22      C:  But you get the smack,=
23      J:  =Yeah.
24          (.)
```

```
        25      C:  .h A:h.=I'm gunna scratch my head there.
        26          (.)
        27      J:  Kuh he:h heh.
        28      C:  That sounds a bit odd.
        29      J:  It does but it's tru:e my mum can't smack my dad so she
        30          puts the anger on me.
        31      C:  A::h.
        32          (1.0)
Q→      33      C:  D'you think she'd prefer to smack dad.
        34          (.)
A→      35      J:  No:.
        36          (0.8)
        37  →   J:  Cuz dad would smack her back an' then, .h they'd have a
        38          big fight on smacking.
        39      C:  A big smacking fight.
        40      J:  Yeah.=
        41      C:  =That doesn't sound like a ver[y nice (thing)
        42  →   J:                                [No: so I just take the
        43  →       smack an' I don't really care (cuz) she can't- .hh well
        44  →       she can smack really hard but it doesn't hu:rt.
F→      45      C:  So::, so 'f she smacks you::, (.) sometimes it might feel
        46  →       better cuz it means that mum and dad don't have a row.
        47      J:  Yeh.
        48      C:  A:::h. 'Ka::y.
```

I have already commented on the occasional use of newsmarkers such as 'Oh' and 'Ah' by counsellors. In this extract, we find the repeated use of such items, often in an exaggerated form, as in 'A::h 'kay'; 'A::h.'; or 'A:::h. 'Ka::y.'. The particles 'Oh' and 'Ah' in turn-initial position are often referred to as change-of-state markers, following Heritage (1984), who found that in ordinary conversation, they tend to be placed in a third slot after question-answer sequences where speakers have either been informed of something or have accomplished repair on a prior misunderstanding. Notably, however, Heritage (1984: 336) remarked that forms of institutional discourse that are characterised by question-answer sequences (medical consultations, interviews, classroom interactions and so on) 'are marked by the absence of "oh" as a routine third-turn receipt object', an absence that 'contributes to the maintenance and reproduction within the talk that it is some special institutionalised activity which is in progress' (original emphasis).

Given this absence of overt newsmarkers in other forms of institutional talk, the question arises as to what this type of turn design is doing in the context of child counselling interaction. Practical manuals caution against the use of responses that can be perceived as evaluations or judgements of the child's talk. Instead they recommend the use of what they call 'minimal responses': 'expressions such as "Ah-ha", "Uh-hum", "Yes", "OK" and "Right"' (Geldard and Geldard 1997: 58). In ordinary conversation, such items can be used as continuers (Schegloff 1982) which exhibit that the recipient of a current extended utterance is both (a) attentive to that utterance and (b) passing on any opportunities to take a turn of their own during its course. Geldard and Geldard (1997: 58) recommend such items because they 'are very useful in encouraging the child to continue to tell his story'. They go on to state that:

> It is important when making . . . minimal responses that they are not likely to be interpreted as judgemental in either a positive or a negative way. If the child is to tell her story accurately, then the story must not be significantly influenced by the child's perception of the counsellor's approval or disapproval. (Geldard and Geldard 1997: 58)

We find here evidence of the model of the counsellor as a neutral conduit, referred to earlier. The assumption is that the child is in possession of their 'story' and the role of the counsellor, as an active listener, is to enable that story to emerge in its authenticity, that is, without distortion. In the present data, however, young children invariably refrain from volunteering information about potentially therapeutic matters. Nevertheless counsellors tend to orient to children's utterances as if they are possible indices of such matters as problematic parental relationships, feelings of anger, guilt or confusion, and so forth. One issue then is how to indicate that there may be something potentially interesting in the child's talk without 'leading' the child.

Newsmarkers like 'Ah' can facilitate this work. A key difference between continuers of the kind recommended by Geldard and Geldard (1997) and newsmarkers is that the former are, indeed, relatively neutral turn components. In as much as they are 'passing' turns, they avoid commenting on the content of an interlocutor's utterance. Newsmarkers, on the other hand, specifically flag up that something of note, some new information, something 'commentable' has been identified in the other person's talk. But at the same time, the newsmarker itself does not specify precisely what it is that may be noteworthy in the prior turn. Through their use, therefore, counsellors can exhibit the extent to which the child's turns provide them with information previously unknown, without directly evaluating any specific part of the child's turn.

Extract (5) above shows how newsmarkers, produced as part of a three-part Q-A-'Ah' structure, can produce the environment in which feelings-talk is elicited by the counsellor via a stepwise technique that culminates in the formulation of therapeutically-relevant matters. In the course of the extract C works to mark out a whole series of newsworthy utterances in a performance of 'discovery' which is ultimately formulated in terms of feelings and consequences on the child's part.

For example, the 'A̱::h' in line 9 comes in response to J's answer to the initial question about whether her playing on the computer would lead to the two parents arguing with each other (lines 1–5). The answer presents a slightly different 'take' on the situation, in which J would argue with each parent individually, and they in turn would 'te̱ll each other off but they wouldn't a̱rgue' (lines 6–8). C's turn-initial newsmarker orients to this as potentially informative, and he appears next to be initiating a follow-up question on the topic, 'Is that, di̱fferent . . .' (line 9). Although this utterance is not ultimately completed, the key point is nevertheless that the newsmarker serves to flag up something potentially informative in the child's prior talk.

C's turn is abandoned as J overlaps the question (line 10) with a follow-up comment of her own, revealing that her mother would 'smack [J] an' send [her] up t'be̱d'. This remark leads to a sequence of exchanges in which the counsellor produces a slightly playful act of 'puzzlement' over this reported situation. In a series of turns between lines 12–28, C seeks to foreground an interpretation of the circumstances which led to the smack as 'a bit o̱dd' (line 28). Here, the newsmarkers in lines 20 and 25 come to play a role in accentuating that very oddness. The first of these occurs in a Q-A-'Ah' structure in which the question, 'She'd smack yo̱u?' is responded to with 'Ye̱ah' (lines 16, 18). The 'A̱:h' is designed to mark this answer as puzzling, as indicated by the latched, disjunctive follow-up statement, 'But she's cro̱ss with da̱d.' In line 25, following a turn which once again foregrounds that it is nevertheless J who 'get(s) the sma̱ck' (line 22, responded to affirmatively in line 23), the 'A̱:h' marks out C's 'puzzlement' even more explicitly, followed as it is with the utterance 'I'm gunna scratch my he̱ad there.'

This segment revolves around another key child counselling trope, in which children are depicted as suffering the consequences of parents' frustrations with each other, as they 'take it out on' the child. In a particularly striking utterance, J herself verbalises this trope as she reacts to the counsellor's 'puzzled' act: 'it's tru:e my mum can't smack my da̱d so she puts the a̱nger on me̱' (lines 29–30).[5] Noticeably, rather than responding to this statement by, say, agreeing that that is indeed what seems to be going on here, the counsellor produces a newsmarker: 'A̱::h.' (line 31). As in the preceding instances (albeit, this time, after a pause (line 32)) the newsmarker is

---

5. Whether C's 'acting puzzled' here represents a strategy for getting the child to see what might be wrong in the circumstances being described is an interesting possibility, but one whose investigation would take us outside the scope of the present chapter. However, if this sequence can indeed be seen as an instance of a more widely adopted strategy, or technique, then it is particularly successful in this case as it results in the child herself verbalising the 'counselling-relevant' interpretation of events. In any case, J's utterance in lines 29–30 is a fine example of just how socially competent children can be seen to be in this kind of institutional setting (recall the discussion in Chapter 1).

followed up by an utterance which seeks to develop the newsworthy aspect that it indexes in the prior turn. The child's responses are then formulated by the counsellor in a way which foregrounds the therapeutically relevant elements of the preceding exchange.

In line 33 C asks, 'D'you think she'd prefer to smack dad', a question which generates a series of responses in which the child first provides a straightforward answer ('No:', line 35); then expands on this by proposing that C's suggestion would mean that her mother and father would begin fighting each other (lines 37–8). Ultimately she indicates that, as a result, J stoically 'take(s) the smack' which, though her mother can 'smack really hard', 'doesn't hu:rt' (lines 42–4). It is following these expansions, or accounts for her initial answer, that C produces a 'so'-prefaced formulation: 'so 'f she smacks you::, (.) sometimes it might feel better cuz it means that mum and dad don't have a row.'

This formulation exhibits a number of key properties that link it to the particular contingencies of the child counselling session. First, it refers the issue under discussion back to the child by reference to her feelings. That is, the issue of the different ways her parents might react to her 'playing on the computer' is described in terms of the child 'feeling better' if she is smacked by the mother. Second, relatedly, it refers this issue to its consequences for the child in terms of child-parent relationships. That is, taking the smack might 'feel better' because it leads to the positive consequence of avoiding a row between mother and father. Third, it picks up on another trope often found in storybooks and other literature, and related to the 'conflicting messages' trope mentioned earlier, in which children are depicted as feeling responsible for their parents' falling out, leading to situations in which they try to intervene to smooth things over, despite the fact that, in this case, it may lead to them 'taking the smack'.

In summary, then, the presence of newsmarkers may perform interactional work which is closely linked to the institutional requirements of child counselling; namely, the elicitation of feelings-talk in an environment where the child rarely volunteers to topicalise such talk yet where counsellors orient to a professional requirement not to act in a way that might be construed as 'leading' the child.

Formulations and the resistance to counselling talk

One thing that emerges from the discussion in the previous sections is that, to a significant extent, the process of formulating therapeutically-relevant matters is dependent on the child's willingness to go along with the counsellor's formulation. However, research in other settings involving children has indicated that such willingness is not to be taken for granted. For example, in Marlaire and Maynard's

(1990) study of standardised educational testing, they found that children frequently react with resistance towards repetitions of their prior talk when produced by adult professionals. Along similar lines, Aronsson and Cederborg (1996) found that children in family therapy settings recurrently reject or resist parents' or professionals' formulations of their 'problems'.[6]

In the present data there are no examples of children overtly rejecting or disagreeing with counsellor formulations of their prior talk. There are, however, examples in which children appear resistant on a broader level to counsellors' attempts to topicalise possible concerns about family relationships. In one particular case (discussed at greater length in Chapter 6), the child ('Peter', 6) systematically resisted any of the counsellor's attempts to topicalise concerns. His principal device in this was to respond to the majority of what the counsellor said, asked, or invited him to do with the words 'Don't know'. Observing the data reveals that, in some cases (though by no means all), the talk that occasions resistance involves the counsellor attempting to produce a formulation. Following are some examples.

As we join extract (6), C is attempting to explore P's feelings in relation to another 'conflicting messages'-type issue. This time, P and his younger brother (the 'Graham' referred to in line 23) had been given differing reasons why their father had changed his mind about taking them on a trip to Paris and instead was going there with his new girlfriend:

(6)   C23/99.3B:B
1   C: That's gonna be sad isn' it when your dad's there an'
2   you're not there with him.
3   (1.5)
4   P: °Thass Josephine.°
5   C: Is that yuh dad'[s girl]friend.
6   P: [(   )]
7   P: (Look.)
8   (.)
9   C: Is it y' dad's girlfriend.
10   P: Yeh.
11   (0.9)
12   C: So is yuh dad still goin' there wi'Josephine.
13   (1.8)
14   P: Yeah,=

---

6. Family therapy is different from child counselling in that the therapist or counsellor sees the parents and children together, in contrast to child counselling where children are seen on their own while parents wait elsewhere. For a discussion of family therapy see, for example, Boscolo et al. (1986).

```
            15     C: =Yeah.
            16        (7.5)
Q→   17     C: Are they takin' any other kids.
            18        (7.9) ((During pause P shakes his head: see line 21))
A→   19     P: °°Don't know.°°
            20        (2.6)
     21 →   C: You already said no:, e-too late yih shook y' head.
            22        (1.0)
F→   23     C: .hh So they're gunna be in Paris without you an'
            24        Peter-Graham,
            25     P: Don't know,
     26 →   C: .hh An' you're gunna be stuck in ↑London.
            27     P: Don't know,
```

C, it appears, is trying to draw out P's feelings or concerns about having been let down by his father. In lines 1–2 he produces an utterance which offers a feelings-relevant interpretation of the situation: that it will be 'sad ... when your dad's there an' you're not there with him'. The child does not verbally respond to this turn; rather, carrying on with the drawing he is making, he adds a picture of the father's girl-friend and points it out to the counsellor ('Thass Josephine', line 4). C subsequently uses this mention of Josephine to pursue the topic of the rearranged Parisian trip. He asks whether Josephine is accompanying P's father (line 12); then, following P's confirmation (line 14), asks whether they are 'takin' any other kids' (line 17). Notably, at the same time as the the child says 'Don't know' (line19) in response to this, he has also produced a non-verbal response, a lateral head-shake, to which the counsellor orients in line 21: 'You already said no:, e-too late yih shook y' head'. This utterance should be understood in the context of a series of attempts by the counsellor to persuade the child to desist in his repetitious avoidance strategy of saying 'Don't know' (described in Chapter 6). One of those attempts has involved a game the object of which is to 'try and get the other person not to say "Don't know",' for instance by asking questions with 'obvious' answers such as 'Would you like a million pounds?' The fact that the counsellor here proposes that the child has been 'caught' shaking his head 'no' at the same time as saying 'Don't know' has echoes of that earlier activity.

Therefore, C's turn in line 21 places 'on the record' a non-equivocal answer to his question in line 17, in place of the equivocal response that P has verbalised in line 19. The fact that the child has thereby confirmed (if only, as it were, by proxy) that the father and girlfriend are visiting Paris alone provides the context in which C can produce a formulation which may be designed to bring into view possible concerns about having been 'left behind'. Note that having heard C embark upon his formulation ('So they're gunna be in Paris without you an' Peter-Graham,' (C first getting the name of P's brother wrong and repairing his reference to 'Graham')), P reinstitutes the strategy he has been using to resist the counsellor's topics throughout the session so far: that is, the repetition of 'Don't know'. In line 26, nevertheless, C presses on with the attempt to elicit feelings-talk, indexing the matter back to the child's feelings through a reference to him being 'stuck in London'.

Extract (7) provides another example, from the same session, of a formulation which occasions resistance from P. This time, the utterance 'Don't know' seems more overtly resistant in the sense that the child shouts the words with an almost palpable anger (line 9):

(7)   C23/99.3B:B
Q→   1   C: Dju think it should stay the sa:me, .h or dju think it
         2   should be diff'rent tuh how it is now.
         3   (1.0)
A→   4   P: °Diff'rent.°
         5   C: Diff'rent.
         6   (1.8)
F→   7   C: So you know it needs to be diff'rent,
         8   (.)
         9 → P: DON'T KNOW!
        10   (.)
        11 → C: No no-n-listen you know it needs t' be diff'rent,
        12   P: Don't kno[w,
        13 → C: [But dju know how it should be.

C's question in lines 1–2 seeks the child's view on the current situation, in which his parents live apart and are not on friendly terms, asking whether this situation (the 'it' referred to) should perhaps be different. The question adopts a form common in the data, whereby counsellors tend to phrase questions in terms of disjunctive alternatives (as in 'Is that good or not so good?', 'Do you like that or do you not like that?' or, here, 'Should it stay the same or should it be different?').[7] One interactional function of disjunctive questions is to encourage the respondent to make an active choice between the proffered alternatives. Clearly, like any question, they can also be responded to with the non-committal 'Don't know'. Note here, however, that P does respond by choosing one of the alternatives (line 4). As in the previous

---

7. Examples of this question form can be found in some of the extracts previously discussed: for instance, in extract (1), lines 14–15 ('So::, (1.8) What bits o' that do y' like an' what bits o' that don't y' like'); and in extract (2), lines 28–9 ('Is 'e gunna learn to shout d'y' think like other teachers. (.) Or d'you think he'll always not shout').

extract, this answer provides C with resources for further talk on the topic which 'Don't know' would systematically withhold, and he uses that opportunity to formulate the child's talk: 'So you kn<u>ow</u> it needs t' be diff'rent' (line 7). One thing to notice here is the way in which the formulation shifts from what the child 'thinks' ('dju think it should be diff'rent', lines 1–2) to what he 'knows' ('So you kn<u>ow</u> it needs t' be di<u>ff</u>'rent', line 7). The formulation thus seeks to foreground knowledge of some need for change, which then provides C with the framework for his follow-up question, 'But dju kn<u>ow</u> how it should <u>be</u>' (line 13). However, once again, it appears that on hearing C beginning a formulation, P judges that he may have 'given away too much' in admitting that things should be 'different'. As in extract (5), his interjected '<u>D</u>ON'T KN<u>OW</u>!' attempts (this time somewhat more forcefully) to reinstate his adopted stance of non-committal resistance.[8]

I remarked at the start of this section that child resistance to, or disagreement with, counsellor formulations is rare in the current data corpus. There are in fact no examples of outright rejection of formulations by the children in my data. Indeed, even in the examples cited above, it is not unequivocally clear whether the child in question is exhibiting resistance to the counsellor's formulations or resistance on a broader level to the overall counselling agenda of discussing problematic family relations. What these examples do illustrate, however, is the way that counsellors may seek to pursue the formulation of therapeutically-relevant matters even when the child exhibits resistance to moving the talk in such a direction. This suggests both the strength of child counsellors' orientation to the need for such matters to be identified and translated from the intra- to the interpersonal sphere; and, more importantly, an orientation to the functionality of formulations in the accomplishment of this work.

Conclusion

This chapter has addressed certain elements of the practice of 'active listening', as found in the child counselling data. Within counselling psychology, the term is usually taken to refer to the ways in which counsellors seek to show responsivity to what the client is saying. I have shown how the conversational practice of 'formulation' is utilised to achieve some of the complex interactional work involved in active listening. Specifically, I discussed how this practice is bound up in the construction of the child as an 'object of therapy'—that is, as someone for whom cer-

---

8. The fact that the counsellor orients to the child's turn here as an interjection can be seen in the way that he repeats the formulation in line 11, that is, following the child's '<u>D</u>ON'T KN<u>OW</u>!' and prior to the counsellor's own production, in line 13, of the follow-up question.

tain counselling-relevant problems or issues apply, even where those may not have been apparent from the content of the child's talk itself.

Fomulations have been shown to be a key resource by means of which children's concerns or feelings about events in their family life are rendered into publicly available topics of talk. Children mostly enter the arena of child counselling at the volition of their parents, and this may account for the fact that the data reveal varying levels of reluctance to actively topicalise family concerns, a reluctance that goes across the 4–12-year age range. Nevertheless, the principles of active listening seem to encourage child counsellors to orient to children's talk as if it contains indexes of concerns that remain unspoken. Formulation, as a technique which generally involves the speaker foregrounding the gist or upshot of a co-participant's talk, is a means by which counsellors can 'reveal' such unspoken concerns; and crucially, this can be done regardless of whether or not the child 'actually' had such concerns lurking in his or her head prior to the formulation.

The analysis has shown how formulations perform 'translations' of a child's talk into therapeutic objects: in other words, recasting it in terms that may be amenable to a counselling intervention. The characteristic properties of such formulations are: (1) that they refer issues back to the child, especially in terms of their subjective experience; (2) that they refer issues to feelings the child has or concerns that they may harbour; and (3) that they refer issues to their consequences in terms of child-parent relationships. These three key properties are what makes the formulations analysed in this chapter particularly 'counselling-relevant'. They are centrally involved in what I have called the elicitation of feelings-talk: the bringing of (possibly unarticulated) intrapersonal phenomena into the interpersonal sphere.

CHAPTER 6

'I don't know'

The interactional dynamics of resistance and response

Child counselling is akin to other forms of counselling and psychotherapy in that it is underpinned by an institutionalised incitement to speak (Silverman 1996).[1] But as has been hinted at in various places so far in this book, that institutional imperative is not straightforward and does not always function smoothly. For example, in the organisations studied by Silverman (1996) and by Peräkylä (1995), counselling (for adults) was provided as part of an overall package associated with the provision of an HIV test, rather than specifically being requested or sought out by the client. As a consequence, counsellors were seen to develop a range of strategies for bringing counselling into play in the face of resistance from the client. Related issues were addressed by Heritage and Sefi (1992) in their study of 'health visitors', qualified nurses who monitor the progress of mothers—particularly first-time mothers—in the weeks following the birth of their child by visiting them at home. In visits carried out at the volition of the health visitor rather than at the request of the mother, a context emerges in which unsolicited advice or counselling on matters of child care is vulnerable to being interpreted as criticism by mothers, and sometimes resisted.

In child counselling, the sessions involve young children who may not fully understand or accept the role of the counsellor, and who have often been introduced to the service at the behest of their parent(s) rather than their own volition. Partly as a result of this, there is always a danger of their active resistance to the production of talk about therapeutic matters. This danger is recognised by counselling practitioners. Geldard and Geldard (1997: 71) remark that children 'tend to avoid emotional pain', and that when issues that are associated with emotional trauma get brought into their awareness, for instance through discussion in counselling, children may 'deflect' those issues. 'This deflection may involve the child becoming silent and withdrawn, or may involve the child distracting away from the painful issues by becoming loud and boisterous' (Geldard and Geldard 1997: 71). However, as already remarked at various points in previous chapters, Geldard and Geldard do not provide any empirical examples of children engaging in this deflection. Similarly, their recommendations as to how counsellors should deal with resistance

---

1. An earlier version of this chapter originally appeared as 'Resisting the incitement to talk in child counselling: Aspects of the utterance "I don't know"', *Discourse Studies*, 4: 147–68 (2002).

are vague—such as 'giving the child feedback' about the resistance or 'validating the child's fear' (1997: 72)—and are equally unsupported by empirical analysis.

In the present chapter, I discuss empirical examples of child resistance and counsellor response found in my data. I focus on a particularly acute case involving a six year old male child in counselling with a male counsellor. The resistance in this case takes neither the silent, withdrawn form nor the loud and boisterous form suggested by Geldard and Geldard (1997). Instead it involves systematic, and often strategic, non-cooperation on the child's part. From early on in the session, the child, anonymised in transcripts as 'Peter', develops a way of avoiding talking about the counsellor's topics by saying, and thenceforth repeating, the words 'Don't know'. In all, throughout the main body of this session, the counsellor asks a total of 92 questions[2] and Peter says 'Don't know' 57 times (note, however, that not all 'Don't know's stand as answers to questions, and not all questions actually get answers). Perhaps a more telling raw statistic is that out of a total of 132 turns taken by Peter during the main counselling dialogue, some 43.5% (57 turns) comprise purely and simply of the words 'Don't know'.

The analysis focuses both on the child's resistance strategy itself, and on the counsellor's techniques for attempting to combat resistance and work towards a therapeutically relevant outcome to the session in question. It has been noted that child resistance to the agendas of adult professionals in settings such as clinics (Silverman 1983, 1987) or school parent–teacher interviews (Silverman, Baker and Keogh 1998) can be treated not as a deficiency on the part of the child but as a display of interactional competence. 'This is because silence [for example] allows children to avoid implication in the ... adult moral universe and thus ... enables them to resist the way in which an institutional discourse serves to frame and constrain their social competencies' (Silverman, Baker and Keogh 1998: 220). The use of 'I don't know' instantiates particular interactional skills in this respect, since it is a recognisable answer to a question, yet builds into the question-answer sequence the possibility that the same answer can be used in response to a follow up request for specification or elaboration.[3] At the same time, by analysing the way that the adult professional develops different responses to this strategy the present chapter adds to our understanding of the practices, discursive techniques and competencies of child counsellors themselves.

---

2. For the purposes of this rough statistical count, I identified as questions only those turns that were syntactically formed as such. See Schegloff (1984) for a more sophisticated take on what counts (interactionally) as a question.

3. See Sacks (1992 Vol. 1: 49–56) for a discussion of how the power of question-answer sequences lies in the way that the questioner gets the right to speak in the next turn following the answer, and in that turn he or she may produce a follow-up question, a situation which Sacks refers to as the 'chaining rule'.

'I don't know' as an interactional object

Utterances disclaiming knowledge, such as 'Dunno', 'I dunno' and 'I don't remember', have been addressed in a range of ways in the discourse analytic and conversation analytic literature (Drew 1989, 1992; Potter 1996b). The main argument pursued in these studies is an interactionist and (broadly) constructivist one that maintains that a speaker's use of words such as 'I don't know' should not be treated purely cognitively, that is, as a literal indication that the speaker 'does not know' something. It is not necessarily, and certainly not only, a report on the mental 'state' of 'lacking knowledge'. Rather, considered within the context of talk-in-interaction, it has to be analysed for the kinds of interactional work it is doing in the sequential places in which it is produced.

For example, Potter (1996b) offers some observations on the use of 'I don't know' produced as a tag at the end of a knowledge claim (in the extract below, a claim about the length of skirt the speaker's wife had been wearing during the events he is describing). The interesting thing about this is that, having first made a claim to knowledge of the state of affairs in question, the speaker appears immediately to be disavowing that knowledge. However, Potter argues that we need not see this in any strictly cognitive sense. Rather, he suggests that the use of 'I don't know' in this kind of tag position functions interactionally as a means of 'inoculating' the speaker against possibly negative inferences that may be drawn on the basis of what he has just said.

Consider extract (1):

(1) From Potter 1996b: 131
    Jimmy: Connie had a short skirt on I don't know . . . .

The extract comes from a recording of a counselling session between a husband and wife concerning problems in their relationship which apparently stem from his jealousy and possessiveness. Jimmy's observation about the length of his wife's skirt is made when he is recalling one specific incident in a longer narrative in which he claims that Connie flirts with other men.

Potter (1996b: 131–2) suggests that the speaker here is in an inauspicious environment: the points he wants to raise have a sensitive character in that they could be the basis for negative assessments about his character. That is, Jimmy is potentially laying himself open to accusations of pathological jealousy. However, we can notice that this observation about the length of his partner's skirt is produced in tandem with an expression of uncertainty: 'I don't know'. This might seem an entirely casual supplement, but for Potter, its use allows the speaker to establish that he has no 'stake' in, or commitment to, the sensitive issues that have been introduced.

In other words, Jimmy's use of 'I don't know' portrays him as not really noticing his wife's dress precisely at the point in the account when it becomes an issue for him. A sceptical recipient of his account might attribute a negative motive to Jimmy for making the 'short skirt' observation: that he is unwarrantably jealous and possessive, and therefore he would have a stake in monitoring the length of his wife's skirt. But by using 'I don't know' to characterise his uncertainty about, or indifference to, his wife's clothes, he is able to inoculate himself against the charge that the grounds for his grievances are not derived from his partner's actual behaviour, but are more a reflection of his own psychological problems.

The point is that it is not necessary to consider whether Jimmy is making any actual disavowal of the knowledge that he has just previously avowed. Produced in this kind of sequential position and in this particular interactional environment, the utterance 'I don't know' does the interactional work which Potter (1996b) characterises as 'stake inoculation' regardless of whether Jimmy really does or does not know (or remember) whether his wife's skirt was short or not.

On the face of it, this tag-positioned use of 'I don't know' is very different from the same utterance's use in a stand-alone turn, such as in response to a question or an invitation. For one thing, in the latter environment, 'I don't know' can comprise the whole of a turn, rather than being tagged onto a prior phrase. For another, the turn in which it is produced is hearable as a response to the interlocutor's previous turn, with the result that its cognitive aspect is open to being treated as an answer to the previous turn's substantive action (the question or invitation). However, Drew (1992) showed how 'I don't know' or 'I don't remember', used in response to an attorney's questions by a witness in court, can have interactional functions that are markedly similar to those claimed by Potter (1996b) for the tag-positioned version.

In analysing the testimony of the female victim of an alleged rape, Drew (1992) notes that the witness frequently uses 'I don't know' or 'I don't remember' in response to the cross examining attorney's questions about details of the night on which the alleged rape took place. For instance, the attorney asks about 'whether or not the tavern was open, whether there were any cars parked in the area, how many telephone calls the defendant made to her, how far he was across the street, whether his car had a spoiler, and so forth' (Drew 1992: 483–4):

(2)   From Drew 1992: 482
    1   Attorney: About how far awa:y was the defendant from you
    2   when you had this conversation?
    3   (0.5)
    4   Attorney: In [feet (.) if you can estimate it
    5   Witness: [(I d-)
    6→ Witness: I don't kno:w how many feet

(3) From Drew 1992: 482–3
```
 1    Attorney:   How many pho̱ne ca:lls would you say that you
 2                (.) had received from the defendant. betwee:n
 3                (0.6) February and June twenny ninth:,
 4                (1.1)
 5 →  Witness:    Ah don' know.
 6                (0.7)
 7    Witness:    Ah didn't answer all of them.
 8                (0.8)
 9    Attorney:   'Scuse me?
10 →  Witness:    Ah do̱n't reme̱mber,=I̱ didn't answer all of them.
```

Drew (1992: 480–6) argues that, regardless of whether the witness actually does or does not remember these small details, stating that she does not know or remember accomplishes specific interactional work. That is, her responses portray these details as unmemorable at the time, as unnoticed, not the sort of thing that she, or perhaps anyone, would feel were worthy of any particular attention. The upshot of this, in the context of the attorney's questions about the alleged rape, is that the witness can exhibit her innocence of the intentions of the alleged rapist, thereby situating herself in the position of a victim who had no reasonable grounds for suspecting that, when she climbed into the man's car to accept a lift, she was about to be sexually assaulted.

In one sense, then, there is a similarity between Drew's (1992) account and Potter's (1996b) idea of stake inoculation: the witness in extracts (2) and (3) is inoculating herself against the potential accusation that she should have suspected something was wrong and that, in not doing so, she was possibly complicit in the alleged rape. As well as advancing this account, Drew considers other non-cognitive, interactional uses of the utterance 'I don't know': for instance, as a strategic device used in order to frustrate a particular line of questioning. Significantly, however, Drew departs from Potter's strict anti-cognitivism by acknowledging that, in some respects, we should continue to bear in mind the specifically cognitive claims embodied in utterances like 'I don't know' or 'I don't remember'.

In the present chapter, I will draw on both these kinds of account. I agree that we cannot treat 'I don't know' straightforwardly as a cognitive claim, and in line with a more interactionist position I will analyse the means by which 'Peter' in my data uses the utterance as a way of strategically avoiding answering certain questions and talking about certain topics. Nonetheless, I also agree with Drew (1992) that we should not deny the fact that 'I don't know' can act as—and be oriented to as—a claim to an actual cognitive state. But I argue that that cognitive claim itself needs to be seen as produced and sustained within the flow of talk-in-interaction.

In order to show this I focus on the ways in which the counsellor himself orients to Peter's use of 'I don't know': first by seeking to treat it (non-cognitively) as a game; then by developing a (cognitive) understanding of it as, in itself, a distinctive therapeutic matter.

The child's strategy: 'Don't know' as a way of avoiding answering

The following two extracts give a first sense of how 'Don't know' is brought into play in specific sequential environments. In both cases, the child is interacting reasonably happily with the counsellor, until it becomes clear that the counsellor is asking particular types of questions: ones that pursue the topic of the falling-out of the child's parents. At that point Peter uses 'Don't know' in overlapping position as an apparent attempt to shut down that line of questioning. It is worth noting that, of the 57 occurrences of 'Don't know' in the session, only four are produced in overlap. Of these, only the two examples discussed below overlap the counsellor's turn by more than two syllables. And in each of these two cases, the 'Don't know' is enunciated brusquely. All this seems to give added weight to the claim that the child is using 'Don't know' to close down a line of questioning.

Consider the arrowed turn in extract (4). The extract begins in the course of a discussion about a drawing the child is producing:

```
(4)  C:23/99.3b:B
    1   P:   That's your bottom.
    2   C:   MY bott[o:m,
    3   P:          [mhuh hah hih hih! .hh! .hh! hih=hih!=
    4   C:   =Is my bottom [that bi:g?
    5   P:                 [.hh! hah .hh! eehih! hrrk!=
    6   C:   =Nyo[::!
    7   P:       [hihih ha hihih! .h!=.hhhh!
    8   C:   What am I doing.=
    9   P:   =.h!=.hhhh!
   10        (0.8)
   11   P:   (Cappring.) (.) I['ve (only) drawn your poo.
   12   C:                    [Uh?
   13        (.)
   14   C:   W- (.) Maybe it sometimes feels like I am a bit pooey. Maybe
   15        coming here, (.) .h feels like it's pooey an' messy an'
   16        horrid.
   17        (2.6)
```

```
18    C:  Yea:h.
19        (2.8)
20    C:  Cuz I make you ta:lk an' think about things that feel pooey
21        don't I.
22        (1.2)
23    P:  POOoo::!=
24    C:  =I make you talk about, (.) mum an' dad not livin' together.
25        (0.8)
26    C:  Mu:m [an' dad fighting.
27 →  P:       [Don't know,
28        (.)
29    P:  Don't know,
30        (.)
31    C:  'N that's sometimes >pooey.<=What uh- what's happening
32        here with my hands.
```

This extract comes from towards the end of the session. P has been drawing a picture for some time, and suddenly announces that what he has just added is a depiction of C's 'bottom'. As C responds with mock indignation, P laughs extensively (lines 3–11). However, from line 14 onwards C begins to construct an interpretation of P's drawing which focuses on the relevance of the counselling setting. And when, in lines 24 and 26, he raises the issue of the child's supposedly problematic family life ('mum an' dad not livin' together . . . Mu:m an' dad fighting'), P attempts to interrupt (line 27) with a strategy that he has, by this stage, been using repeatedly throughout the session, the slightly clipped enunciation of 'Don't know'. Some evidence of C's orientation to this as a 'closing down' move on P's part may be provided in lines 31–2, where he rather swiftly terminates of the topic of how 'pooey' counselling can be and 'rushes through' (indicated by the equals sign at the transition relevance place after 'pooey') into a new topic, referring again to the drawing in front of them ('what's happening here with my hands').

Extract (5) shows a similar use of 'Don't know' in overlapping position as a way of orienting to the undesirability of C's line of questioning:

```
(5)   C:23/99.3b:B
 1    C:  Dju think mum and dad er ever gonna get on again.=dju think
 2        they're ever gonna- .hh say things that're nice to each
 3        other,
 4        (0.9)
 5    C:  Never?
 6        (.)
 7    P:  Yeah never-
```

```
8     C: Never ever ever?
9     P: Never ever ever EVer.=
10    C: =Can you remember when they, (.) u:sed to say nice things to
11       each other,
12       (.)
13    P: Mmm, (0.3) a few million years ago,
14    C: Yea:h,
15       (1.8)
16    C: Can you still remember a few million years ago,
17    P: Mm mm,
18       (.)
19    C: Not really,
20    P: No,
21       (2.1)
22    C: Have you ever seen them say nice things to ea[ch other,
23 →  P:                                               [Don't know,
24       (2.0)
25 →  C: A::h, I'm not gonna win this game again am I.
```

Here, P seems to cooperate for a short time with C's topic of whether 'mum and dad er ever gonna ... say things that're nice to each other'. Although P's turns in lines 7, 9 and 13 exhibit features of escalation and exaggeration that have been noted in the combative talk of children of this age (Lein and Brenneis 1978), there is a degree of cooperation as the counsellor asks about P's own opinions and memories about his mother and father. However, the question in line 22 refers specifically to behaviour that P can recall actually seeing, and therefore is more concrete. This is responded to with an overlapping (and audibly brusque) 'Don't know'. In this case, C himself more clearly orients to this as an attempt at closing down the topic when, in line 25, rather than pursuing his own topic, he acknowledges that the child is engaging in the 'game' of avoiding answering.

The strategic, non-cognitive use of 'Don't know' seems particularly clear in these extracts: given that both are taken from the latter stages of the session, the overlapping placement is indicative of the reinstigation of a technique which has previously got P out of talking about problematic issues (see below); while at the same time, C himself evidently orients to the fact that the child is using this move strategically. In both cases, C responds to the production of 'Don't know' by withdrawing from the pursuit of his therapeutically relevant topic (by changing topic in extract 4 and by referring to the 'game' in extract 5). However, this kind of backing down is not the only way in which C reacts to P's avoidance strategy throughout this session. In order to analyse the development of his response, we need to track back to the beginning of the session and observe the way in which the resistance strategy itself emerges.

Extract (6) is taken from very near the beginning of the session, and opens as the counsellor raises some topics they had discussed with the child's mother just prior to the session:

(6) C:23/99.3b:B
```
 1  C:   Okay.=Wait a minute, I want to tell you some things first.
 2       (0.5) Before you start drawing. (0.5) Okay?
 3  P:   Yeh.=
 4  C:   =So I want y' to do that. .hh A::nd d'you remember the
 5       other thing mum, (1.2) talked about?
 6       (0.6)
 7  P:   (A:::t's) um, daddy says we not goin tuh, (1.1) mum says-
 8       Mum s- Daddy says dut mummy says. .hhh dut we can't go
 9       an' dad-[dy-] an' mummy says .h dut we- .h dut daddy says=
10  C:          [Yeh]
11  P:   =we can't go.
12  C:   So::, .h (1.0) Dad, (.) booked a holiday, (1.0) fuh you
13       an::d,
14  P:   mhhh
15  C:   Graha[m,
16  P:        [Graham=no Grayaa.
17  C:   Graya?
18  P:   Yeh.
19       (0.8)
20  C:   It's Graha:m! ((smile voice))
21       (.)
22  P:   No Gray°aa°. (('pleading' voice))
23  C:   Alright Graya. .h So daddy booked a holiday for you and
24       Graya to go to where.
25       (1.0)
26  C:   Disneyland,=
27  P:   =Tuh Disneyland.
28       (.)
29  C:   A:::nd, (1.5) And then he told you that you can't go
30       cuz mummy says you can't go,
31       (0.8)
32  P:   Yeh.
33  C:   An' you then said t'm- asked mummy, (1.0) an' she said
```

34		no that's not tru:e, daddy said-ju can't- daddy, got
35		it wrong.
36		(2.1)
37	C:	Is that right=is that what happened.
38	P:	Yeh.
39	C:	So what-what- what d'you think happened=who- who said
40		you couldn't go.
41		(0.7)
42	P:	Both of them.
43	C:	Bo:th of them,
44		(2.5)
45	C:	Are you surprised they said you couldn't go.
46	P:	Yeah,
47	C:	You are.
48	P:	Mm.
49		(1.0)
50	C:	Why d'you think they said you couldn't go.
51	P:	Mmm don't know,
52		(1.2)
53	P:	Mm wanna start dra:win'.
54	C:	Does- do::, (0.2) the fights that mum and dad have, stop
55		you doing other things.
56	P:	Yea-a[h.
57	C:	[What kind've things d'they stop you doing.
58		(2.4)
59	P:	Mm-ooh I don't know.
60	C:	Mm.
61		(3.8)
62	C:	Why d'you think, (1.8) mum an' dad said what they said.
63		(0.4)
64	P:	Don't know,
65		(4.1)
66	C:	Cuz it sounds like they were a bit cross.
67		(0.6)
68	P:	Don't know,
69	C:	Who d'you think they're cross with.=
70	P:	=Don't kno[w,
71	C:	[.h O:h I think you do:[:, I think you're playing]=
72	P:	[huh huh, .hhh hih hih]
73	C:	=[games with me.

74	P:	[.hhh hih=hih
75		(1.6)
76	C:	Have I got to try an'- .h will you say don't know all
77		ev̲ening.
78		(.)
79	P:	Don't know.
80	C:	Hmm.

The start of this extract provides some context for the session. In lines 4–5, C introduces a topic that 'mum talked about' in their brief chat before the counselling session and invites P to recollect it. P does so in his next turn (lines 7–11), where he presents a somewhat muddled account of the conflicting versions of events provided by his parents concerning a suggested trip to Disneyland. The account is then clarified by C in his subsequent turns. This is significant because, as the extract proceeds, it becomes clear that C has picked up on this as a potentially difficult family-related issue for the child. Indeed, it is a scenario that is frequently represented in books and leaflets aimed at children in separation and divorce, with parents providing mutually conflicting stories and reasons for their actions, thus serving to confuse and distress the child. As such, this little scenario about a proposed, then cancelled, trip to Disneyland can serve the counsellor as a gateway into counselling talk.

However, what also becomes evident is that the further C seeks to pursue the topic of the trip and possible reasons for its cancellation, the more P resists. C puts a series of questions about the Disneyland trip to P following the description of the scenario. Notice that the first few questions, in lines 37, 39, and 45, all receive answers—albeit minimal ones—from P. The first question seeks confirmation of the accuracy of C's account of events, and is answered affirmatively. In line 39 C begins to direct the talk towards the potentially problematic issue at stake: the conflicting accounts offered by P's parents. Of the two questions produced in this turn ('what d'you think happened' and 'who said you couldn't go'), P elects to answer the second one, and to do so, again, minimally and literally: 'Bo̲th of them' said he couldn't go.

C then begins to press for the child's reaction to this circumstance. 'Are you surpr̲ised they said you couldn't go' in line 45 gets another minimal response: 'Yeah.' The next question is a 'why' question and as such does not easily lend itself to the same kind of minimal confirmation or disconfirmation ('Why d'you think they said you couldn't go̲'). Nevertheless, such 'why' questions do have available minimal responses, and P here uses perhaps the most straightforward one, a knowledge disclaimer: 'M̲mm, don't know'.

P's attempt, following this, to move on and start the activity of making a drawing (line 53) is declined by C, who instead pursues his line of questioning. He asks about 'mum and dad's fights' (lines 54 and 57); he then reiterates his earlier question 'Why d'you think [they] s<u>ai</u>d what they said' (line 62); he offers his own interpretation of why they said it by suggesting that mum and dad were 'a bit cr<u>o</u>ss' (line 66). He then again asks P once more to speculate on his parents' motives with 'Who d'you think they're cross with' (line 69). This line of questioning seems to be grounded in a standard trope used in child counselling texts, where parents are often depicted from the child's point of view as being 'cross' with each other, leaving the child stuck in the middle. The counsellor's aim seems to be to get the child to think about where responsibility for his confusion about the Disneyland trip might lie, and presumably (again in line with a standard child counselling procedure) to see that it lies with his parents and not with him.

We can see that the child responds to this series of turns with a series of 'Don't know' turns. The strategic character of this repetitious use of 'Don't know' for resisting the counsellor's line of questioning becomes particularly clear in lines 68–70. Three points are worth noting. First, in line 68, C produces 'Don't know' for the first time in a sequential context following a turn that is not grammatically a question ('Cuz it s<u>ou</u>nds like they were a bit cross', line 66). Second, C follows up this 'Don't know' for the first time without leaving a gap (see previous instances in lines 52, 61 and 65), thereby increasing the tempo of his questioning. And third, the suddenly increased tempo is sustained by P, who produces a further 'Don't know' in a latched position in line 70. The impression here is that both of them increasingly recognise that whatever the counsellor asks, the child will now respond to it with 'Don't know'.

It is at this point that we see the counsellor's first attempt at dealing with the interactional dilemma that is beginning to be posed for him. He treats the child's resistance to his line of questioning as a game. Note, in his utterance at line 71, the playful enunciation, as well as the stated claim that C takes it that the child does know the answers and is actively choosing not to give them. Note also the way in which P himself collaborates in the game interpretation, in his laughter in lines 72 and 74. Following this (in data not shown) the two of them engage for some minutes in a question-and-answer game, the aim of which is to 'try and get the other one not to say "Don't know"'.[4]

We get a strong sense, then, of one kind of strategic, non-cognitive use of 'Don't know' in the child counselling setting—as a means of attempting to close down an undesired line of counsellor questioning by the child. We have seen how the child brings the 'Don't know' strategy into play in specific sequential environments. These environments involve the counsellor aiming to develop collaborative talk on

---

4. The game involves asking questions with answers that are 'obviously' not 'Don't know', such as 'Would you like a million pounds?'.

topics associated with possible therapeutic matters. The use of 'Don't know' emerges very early on in the session as a means of exhibiting resistance to the requirement to talk on those matters. And the counsellor himself orients to the non-cognitive, strategic use of 'Don't know' as something other than a reflection of the child's lack of knowledge on the issues in question.

The counsellor's response: 'Don't know' and the modulation between playful and serious talk

As remarked previously, it is not enough just to treat the utterance 'I don't know' in this strategic, non-cognitive sense. Although the counsellor begins by orienting to it in this way, as the session develops there is a significant sense in which the literal, cognitive aspects of 'knowing' and 'not knowing' come to be bound up in his varying responses to, and eventual therapeutic uses of and possible solution to, the child's repeated use of 'Don't know'.

I have noted that the initial response developed by the counsellor to the child's resistance technique is to adopt a playful stance and turn the repeated saying of 'Don't know' into a game. Nevertheless, it is clear that the playful framework is a temporary one, and the counsellor eventually seeks to direct the talk back towards counselling-relevant topics.[5] At this point, it quickly becomes clear that for the child, the strategy we saw developing in extract (6) above is an effective one that he intends to adopt for the longer term, as the rest of the counselling session plays out and the counsellor continues to solicit talk on the topic of current family issues.

In this dynamic, there develops what I will refer to as a modulation between 'playful' and 'serious' orientations to P's repetition of 'Don't know'. It is this modulation that, we will see, eventually provides the counsellor with an alternative response to the interactional dilemma that is confronting him. We will also see that this ultimate response turns out to be intimately bound up with C's eventual identification of what I described above as a therapeutic matter: the matter that enables the construction of what, for him at least, is evidently a worthwhile therapeutic intervention. In other words, it enables him to salvage the very therapeutic dimension of the counselling session that the child's non-cooperation has placed under threat.

---

5. It is worth pointing out that games of various kinds can in fact be used as tools for doing counselling. The counsellors in my data regularly used a specially designed board game with older children, in which the questions that have to be answered all consist of hypothetical family scenarios. The aim of the 'correct' answers is to help the child to think positively and avoid self-blame, among other things. See also Peräkylä (1995) for a discussion of the importance of hypothetical scenarios in the management of counselling as a specific form of interaction.

The following three extracts all show examples of C attempting to shift P's talk out of the supposedly playful 'Don't know' mode. Extract (7) is taken from a point just after the 'Try to get the other not to say "Don't know"' game referred to above, and shows C once more attempting to topicalise P's reactions to the failed Disneyland trip with which the session started. Extracts (8) and (9) are taken from later, once C has finally abandoned this line and acceded to P's desire to draw pictures.

(7) C:23/99.3b:B
```
1      C: .ht Shall I tuh- I want to talk a little bit about (that) cuz,
2          y'know when um, you just said t'me about mum an' dad en- not
3          being able to go on holiday 'r you disappointed?
4          (.)
5      P: Don't know,
6      C: You can nod'n shake your head you don't have to- say anything.
7      P: Don't know,
8→     C: No go on nod- sit up and nod- nod or shake your head.
9          An' I'll ask y' some questions.
```

(8) C:23/99.3b:B (Child is making a picture involving numbers)
```
1      C: How often do you say don't know in cla:ss.
2      P: Don't know,
3          (0.8)
4      C: Point tuh the numbers.
5          (.)
6      P: Don'[t know,
7→     C:     [On the- on y' la- no jus' point t' the number. On yer lap.
8      P: °Don't know,°
```

(9) C:23/99.3b:B (Referring to the child's drawing)
```
1      C: Is that da:d. in Paris,
2          (2.1)
3      C: Who's this in Paris,
4      P: °Don't know,°
5→     C: No who is it, an-=seriously who is it.
6      P: °Don't know.°
7          (.)
8      C: Jus' people,
9          (1.6)
10     C: °Mm.°
```

In each of the arrowed turns, C attempts to get P to abandon the game and answer the question 'seriously'. The fact that C orients to P's initial 'Don't know' responses to his question as non-serious is evident from the construction of the arrowed turns, which all take the similar form of 'No' plus a repeat of the question or instruction: 'No go on...nod or shake your head', 'no jus' point t' the number', and 'No . . . seriously who is it'. Each time, therefore, C clearly orients to what P is doing as avoiding answering. It is worth noting that in extracts (7) and (8), there is evidence that C may be considering a possible reason for the child's avoidance, namely that he does not want to speak, or is afraid of doing so, in the visible presence of the researcher's tape recorder. Utterances such as 'just nod or shake your head' or 'just point to the number' offer the child a way of answering that is not 'hearable' by the machine (recall the discussion in Chapter 3). Nevertheless, the point is that at this stage C appears to be frustrated by the child's resistance technique and responds by pressing for a shift into serious talk.

However, at certain points in the child's talk we find evidence that, for him, answering with 'Don't know' is itself a way of producing serious talk. In other words, the child occasionally uses 'Don't know' in such a way as to display that he is not playing a game. For instance, in extract (10), P repeats 'Don't know' in response to the pursuit of a question by C, on the second occasion using emphatic, and angry, tones (arrowed):

```
(10)   C:23/99.3b:B
  1      C:  So:, (.) what yih gonna draw at the bottom.=something else
  2          t'tell yuh mum an' dad.
  3      P:  Mm:: don't know,
  4      C:  Somink else t' tell y' mum'n [dad.
  5 →    P:                               [Don't KNOW!
  6          (.)
  7      C:  Have a think.
```

In extract (11), a similarly emphatic enunciation is used at a point where it seems that the counsellor has maneouvred the child into talking about one of the matters he has been avoiding all session: his feelings about 'how things should be' between himself and his parents:

```
(11)   C:23/99.3b:B
  1      C:  Dju think it should stay the sa:me, .h or dju think it
  2          should be diff'rent tuh how it is now.
  3          (1.0)
  4      P:  °Diff'rent.°
  5      C:  Diff'rent.
  6          (1.8)
  7      C:  So you know it needs to be diff'rent,
```

```
         8        (.)
         9→  P:  DON'T KNOW!
        10        (.)
        11   C:  No no-n-listen you know it needs t' be diff'rent,
        12   P:  Don't kno[w,
        13   C:             [But dju know how it should be.
```

Once C has got P to admit that he thinks things should be 'diff'rent' (line 4), he pursues an upshot of that in a two-part format (line 7 and line 13), only for P to interject with a shouted 'DON'T KNOW!' in line 9. Note that, in response to this, C once more brings into play the 'No' plus repeat format seen in extracts (7)–(9), while P once again interjects with a repetition of 'Don't know' (lines 11–13).

These two occurrences are marked out prosodically from the other 55 'Don't know' turns that P produces in this session. All others are produced either in a clipped, almost mechanical style, or as a whisper, or occasionally with a sing-song intonation. In both the above cases, there is an increase in volume and a more pronounced stress pattern, with the result that P's enunciation strongly conveys that he is 'not playing about', that he is serious about 'not wanting to talk about this'.

As I have indicated, it is in this modulation between whether P's 'Don't know's should be taken as playful or as serious that the counsellor eventually finds a solution that enables him to treat this session as, in fact, a successful child counselling event. This solution also turns on a second modulation, between 'Don't know' as a non-cognitive, strategic device, and 'Don't know' as a cognitive state of mind.

The key moment in this comes towards the end of the session when C asks P to write a final message for his parents at the bottom of the picture he has been drawing for most of the session. This is shown in extract (12):

```
(12)    C:23/99.3b:B
         1    C:  Ahw- what yih could draw if y' don't know right, .mhh i::s
         2         (.) yih could draw a picture, .h of how you w:ant it to be
         3         with mum an' dad.
         4         (4.8) ((Sounds of drawing))
         5    C:  Wha's that say?
         6         (1.0)
         7    P:  Don't, (.) know.
         8         (.)
         9→   C:  Ehuh huh huh haah ha n-hee it does doesn' it.=.hhh Can you
        10→        draw a pictur:e, .h- (1.8) Maybe you're tellin' me that's
        11→        how, .hh (.) that's how y- you don't know how it should be
        12→        between mum an' dad.
```

Having been asked to 'draw a p̲icture, .h of how you w:a̲nt it to be with mum an' dad', P in fact writes 'Don't know' (line 7). What is noticeable is how C responds to this, initially, by treating it as playful. He laughs (line 9), then immediately embarks on reiterating his invitation to the child to draw a picture. In the course of this very reiteration, C's sudden realisation of a different way of interpreting P's actions is exhibited in the cut-off inbreath (line 10), followed by a pause, and then the formulation of a new account which now focuses on the possibility that the child, far from avoiding answering, does not in fact know 'how it should be between mum an' dad' (lines 11–12). That is, in this momentary shift exhibited in C's self-repair at line 10, 'Don't know' becomes treated interactionally not as a game or a strategy, but as a state of mind.

Subsequently, the counsellor focuses his talk around the issues of 'knowing', 'not knowing', and the question of who 'should know' and who 'should not know' what is happening in P's life. The final two extracts show how a counselling-relevant interpretation is developed for the repetition of 'Don't know', and how the counsellor thereby finds a positive therapeutic outcome from a session that, until this stage, has seemed in danger of failing in its incitement to produce therapeutic talk.

(13)   C:23/99.3b:B
```
 1      C: Dju know what you want mum an' dad t' do:.=
 2      P: =Don't know,
 3         (1.5)
 4→     C: I beli:eve you I think you don't know. (.) Mm.
 5         (1.1)
 6      C: Does anybody know,
 7         (1.9)
 8      C: Do mum an' dad know,
 9         (4.2)
10      P: (          )
11         (2.6)
12      C: Maybe they don't know. (1.1) Maybe you're right.
13         (5.4)
14      C: Dju know what I:-cuz I thought you were playin' a ga:me
15         sayin' don't know. (.) But I actually think you're right.
16→        Maybe- (.) maybe don't know's the- best word to use at the
17→        moment. (.) Cuz yuh don't know.
18         (2.1)
19      P: Don't know,=
20→     C: =Y'don't know why::, (.) yuh not allowed t' go t' Paris,
```

```
21      P:  Don't know,
22 →    C:  Y'don't know why::, (.) mum an' da:d are fighting so much,
23          (1.5)
24 →    C:  Y'don't know why::, (0.4) yer mum an' dad's houses are so far
25          apa:rt,
26          (0.9)
27 →    C:  Y'don't know why:: you're feeling so sa:d,
28          (3.4)
29 →    C:  You just don't know.
```

In extract (13), C engages in offering an interpretation of P's 'Don't know's which focuses not on avoidance, nor on game-playing, but on the fact that the child is in a situation that is so difficult to understand that not 'knowing' is both entirely understandable, and acceptable. In a series of four identically-intoned turns at lines 20, 22, 24, and 27, he summarises the issues which P has used 'Don't know' to avoid talking about, but this time treating 'Don't know' as an actual state of mind—an interpretation which is emphasised in the terminal 'You just don't know' in line 29.

In the final extract, which follows on from extract (13), C moves on to use a still more 'cognition-based' interpretation of 'knowing' and 'not knowing':

```
(14)    C:23/99.3b:B
    1       C:  An' here's me, (.) tryin' tuh tell you:, (.) that y' should
    2           know. (1.1) An' why should you know. (1.6) You're six years
    3 →         o:ld aren't you. (1.8) How can you know when you're six years
    4           old.
    5           (9.9)
    6       C:  That's taught me a lot today,=thank you.
    7           (3.2)
    8       C:  Thanks Peter I n- .hh I needed that lesson, (0.9) I needed
    9           that lesson (.) about,
   10           (1.8)
   11       P:  Don't know,=
   12       C:  =Don't know's. Yeah.
   13           (1.0)
   14       P:  Don't know,
   15       C:  I'm gunna think about that a lot tonight.
   16           (2.1)
   17       C:  Thank you fuh teaching me that.
   18           (7.9)
   19 →    C:  I tell you who I think should know,
   20           (2.4)
```

21   C: Who should kn<u>ow</u>.
22   (1.8)
23   C: I think i's your mu:m, and your d<u>a</u>d.
24   (4.3) ((Sounds of child drawing))
25 → C: They're thee shu- p<u>e</u>ople 'oo should kn<u>ow</u>.

Here, the child is presented as one who cannot actually be expected to 'know' (lines 1–4). The counsellor then gives a further positive twist to his interpretation by suggesting that P's repetitious 'Don't know's have actually taught him something (lines 6–17). Finally, in lines 19–25, C recruits the cognitive elements of 'knowing' in a suggestion that it is not, after all, the child, but the parents, who 'should know' about the issues that are serving to confuse him.

Thus, faced with the child's persistence in saying, and ultimately writing (extract 12), 'Don't know' in response to questions about why his parents do the things that they do, how he feels about that, and how things should be between his parents and himself, we have seen the counsellor progress through three distinct stages. First, he attempts to treat it as if Peter is playing a game in intentionally avoiding giving the answers that, the counsellor assumes, he does in fact have. Second, the counsellor abandons the game approach and makes a number of attempts to get Peter to be serious and provide the answers that the counsellor orients to him as intentionally withholding. Third, and finally, the counsellor develops a literal way of responding which involves not simply re-framing his understanding of 'Don't know' from the non-cognitive to the cognitive, but doing so in such a way as to use the re-framing as an opportunity to validate the child in his attempts to resist. This is evident in the difference between the counsellor's initial, apparently sceptical response shown in this detail from extract (6):

      C: Who d'you think they're cross with.=
      P: =Don't kno[w,
  →   C: [.h <u>O</u>:h <u>I</u> think you d<u>o</u>::, I think you're
         playing g<u>a</u>mes with me.

and his final response shown in this detail from extract (13):

      C: Dju know what you want mum an' dad t' do:.=
      P: =Don't know,
            (1.5)
  →   C: I beli:eve you I think you don't kn<u>ow</u>. (.) Mm.

Geldard and Geldard (1997: 72) recommend such validation of resistant behaviour as a key strategy by which counsellors can help children to see that 'it is legitimate to feel that way and it is acceptable to respond by withdrawing'. But what we have seen in this analysis is that it is not always immediately clear when children are in fact resisting, or even that they are resisting. The counsellor here is faced with the task of judging, in the course of the counselling session itself, what it is that the child's 'Don't know's are really doing. His initial response, while apparently sceptical, might equally be seen as seeking to validate the child's behaviour by placing it within a game framework. However, it is only towards the end of the session that an alternative form of validation is developed that involves the counsellor avowing belief in, and acceptance of, the child's state of 'not knowing'.

Although there is no evidence in the data that P offers any explicit uptake of this new, affirmational approach to his non-cooperative behaviour—he responds either by continuing to say 'Don't know' or by carrying on with his drawing—there may be some evidence at the end of the session that the counsellor has succeeded in one therapeutic outcome by providing the child with a new resource for managing how he feels about his parents' separation. As they prepare to leave the room, the counsellor suggests that they show the drawing, which depicts the mother and father in their separate houses beneath which the child has written 'Don't know', to the mother who is waiting in a separate room. Quietly, but decisively, the child agrees.

Conclusion

Textbooks and manuals aimed at child counselling practitioners point out that children are prone to resisting the incitement to talk, and offer certain techniques for combatting resistance. However, there is rarely any evidence that discussion of either children's resistance strategies or counsellors' responses are based on empirical observation of naturally occurring child counselling discourse. Whatever information might be offered by such handbooks, therefore, it is important to carry out detailed observational analyses of actual child counselling discourse, as only then can we understand the true richness of the interactional resources brought into play by both counsellors and children in the management of therapeutic interaction as it unfolds.

In this chapter, we have seen how a particular type of resistance to counselling talk is brought into play, and how the counsellor attempts to respond in the course of naturally occurring child counselling interaction. The repeated use of 'Don't know' as a response to questions is a particularly powerful resistance strategy as it is capable of frustrating any line of questioning the counsellor seeks to pursue, while at the same time inoculating the child against being held to account for, or expected to explain or develop, any thoughts or feelings that he might actually have on the matters in question. In this sense, we can see 'Don't know' as a manifestation of the competence of this six year old child in managing an almost total avoidance of the counsellor's therapeutic agenda. By the same token, it poses a serious dilemma for the counsellor in so far as he seeks to pursue that therapeutic agenda while not actually able to force the child to speak on the topics he is trying to raise.

Both counsellor and child must manage this competition in the real time unfolding of talk-in-interaction. The child's adopted strategy is additionally powerful in this respect, since 'Don't know' is an utterance that can be produced in response to virtually any prior turn. Nevertheless, it is testimony to the counsellor's skilfulness in this case that he eventually works out a fruitful way of dealing with that resistance. This ultimately allows the counsellor to salvage at least some aspects of therapeutic relevance for this particular counselling session. In shifting from a non-cognitive to a cognitive interpretation of 'Don't know', he constructs an account for the child's apparent resistance to his attempts to elicit therapeutically relevant talk that comprehends such resistance in terms of a particular interpretive trope used in child counselling. This can be described as the 'parents should sort it out' trope (cf. Geldard and Geldard 1997: 75–6). One of the main concerns pursued in counselling for children in parental separation and divorce is to emphasise that the family break-up is not the child's fault. Responsibility for resolving the problem therefore rests with the parents and not the child. In bringing this trope into play the counsellor is able to validate the child's resistance to counselling talk, and offer the possibility, at least, of an alternative, positive interpretation of the child's unwillingness to collaborate in such talk. At the core of that is a shift in understanding of the meaning and relevance, for this particular, situated interaction, of the status of claims to 'know' and 'not know'.

CHAPTER 7

Child counselling and the incitement to communicate

This book has explored various aspects of the interactional organisation of child counselling, with a specific focus on counselling for young children (between 4–12 years) who are experiencing parental separation or divorce. In Chapter 1, I described the main analytical topics for the book as follows:

- The techniques by which counsellors draw out children's concerns about family trauma.
- The resources children use to make sense of their experience in the light of counsellors' questions.
- The discursive means by which children are situated as therapeutic subjects.
- The means by which children, through talking and avoiding talking, cooperate in or resist their therapeutic subjectification.

Following a methodological overview in Chapter 2, Chapter 3 addressed the dynamic interplay between these features of child counselling in the light of how the recording technology used for data collection was situated as an interactionally relevant phenomenon by both counsellor and child. We saw how the participants' awareness of the technology's presence, which constitutes a methodological concern for many schools of thought in social research, could be analysed as a resource which participants themselves use as part of the situated interactional work of child counselling.

Chapters 4 and 5 examined some key resources used by counsellors in the attempt to draw out of the child therapeutically-relevant talk. On one level, therefore, these chapters were about the discursive construction of children as therapeutic subjects. Yet we also saw how that process is far from straightforward, as children exert their own competencies in declining uptake of counsellors' therapeutic formulations, seek to foreground their own interpretations, or attempt to exercise control over the topical direction of the talk. In Chapter 6, this was brought into sharp focus as counsellor and child battled over the topicalisation or otherwise of therapeutically-relevant matters.

All this suggests that child counselling, far from being simply the kind of therapeutic helping discourse it is often portrayed as, actually involves networks and dynamics of interactional power and resistance. In particular, the means by which children are situated as therapeutic subjects and the means by which children, through talking and avoiding talking, cooperate in or resist their therapeutic subjectification, constitute a terrain on which different resources may be brought to bear to establish hegemony in the local, and constantly evolving, contexts of talk-in-interaction.

In this final chapter I want to bring these issues together in a discussion which will hopefully both highlight and integrate the key themes that have emerged from the preceding detailed empirical analyses, and at the same time indicate the relevance of the book's central findings for its various audiences, including sociologists of language and interaction, childhood, and organisations, and professional child counsellors themselves.

A conversation-analytic take on the professional discourse of child counselling

Although this book has examined phenomena that may be discussed in child counselling textbooks, such as 'therapeutic vision', 'active listening' and 'resistance', my aim has not been to evaluate either the process or the outcomes of child counselling as a professional practice. Such interests are key to much of the work that has been done in counselling psychology in recent years (see for example Woolfe and Dryden 1996). But as Silverman (1996) points out, an emphasis on evaluating either processes or outcomes leads in different ways to a situation in which the phenomenon itself—that is, what actually happens in the counselling session—disappears.

Silverman (1996: 24) observes how a vast amount of counselling research seeks to develop a normative model of good counselling practice which can be assessed using either quantitative measures of 'outcomes' or qualitative measures of people's 'responses' to counselling. In either case,

> research [is] fundamentally concerned with the environment around the phenomenon rather than the phenomenon itself. In quantitative studies of 'objective' social structures and qualitative studies of people's 'subjective' orientations, we may be deflected from the phenomenon towards what follows and precedes it (causes and consequences in the 'objective' approach) or to how people respond to it (the 'subjective' approach).

Consequently, like Silverman, my approach has been to turn the focus not towards what people think about counselling but towards what they *do* in counselling. The aim was not to begin with a normative model of counselling and then evaluate the extent to which the actual practices of counsellors and clients match up with that model. Rather, it has been to describe the practices through which both counsellors and children talk into being the institutional reality of child counselling as a form of social interaction. What these chapters have offered is a sustained, and unique, look inside the child counselling room at the kinds of talk-in-interaction that occur there.

The uniqueness I refer to derives from the methodological orientation of the book. Part of the significance of using conversation analysis is the demand that actual ('naturally occurring') discourse is studied. Hence this marks the research out from other published work on child counselling which has tended to utilise note-taking, recollection or even intuition as its source of information about what goes on within sessions. Such methods are now widely understood to be inadequate, especially for any analysis of language use in actual social interaction.

Studies of counselling and psychotherapy using CA show how a close examination of the ways people talk in such settings can provide valuable insights into the kinds of strategies used by counsellors to help clients make sense of and find ways of dealing with their situations. Those strategies are embedded in, and at the same time constitutive of, patterns of interaction that render the talk recognisably different from ordinary 'casual' conversation; a form of institutional discourse underpinned by the orientation of at least one participant (and much of the time, both) to certain tasks.

The task-oriented nature of the interaction was described, in Chapter 2, as a characteristic feature of institutional discourse generally. We saw how 'non-formal' types of institutional interaction such as child counselling are organised according to bricolage practices that result in distinctive patterns in the talk and participation of different role incumbents. However, we have also seen that child counselling has a distinctive character which derives from the particular interactional, social and ideological dynamics which frame its professional concerns.

For one thing, as described in Chapter 1, the discourse of child counselling is situated at an interface between the growing recognition of children's social competence and agency (James and Prout 1990; Hutchby and Moran-Ellis 1998), and an increasing trend that favours the importance of 'good communication' as a means of improving social organisation and solving social problems (Cameron 2000). Chapter 1 introduced the competence paradigm in sociological studies of childhood, and also discussed related legal developments that foreground children's own views in matters affecting their lives. I argued that the increasing presence of child counselling practices in modern towns and cities can to some extent be linked to those new directions in our views of childhood. In particular, child counselling sessions appear to present an important opportunity for children experiencing family separation (or other traumatic events) to speak of their experience in their own words. Indeed, this is the way that many counsellors themselves conceive of the work they do.

But throughout the book, what we have seen is that in child counselling, the competencies that children display in their talk and other associated activities are situated in, and sometimes constrained by, the context of the adult-driven, professionalised discourses of counselling as a 'helping discourse'. This has consequences for the nature of the talk that occurs during sessions; for the structure of children's participation in sessions; and for the professional work of the child counsellor as it takes place within sessions.

One way of encapsulating this is by reference to a twin set of paradoxes that come into play to shape child counselling discourse along certain dimensions. On one level, the event itself and its characteristic forms of talk are paradoxical from the child's perspective. The talk produced by counsellors places them in the category of 'child' in as much as they are viewed in relation to their parents, whose actions have consequences for them as children. However, the task-orientation of counsellors within the setting ultimately means that children are routinely invited to speak in ways that are outside the normative parameters of 'childhood' as it tends to operate in the context of child-adult interaction, for instance by speculating on their parents' reasoning, articulating their own feelings and responses to their parents' actions, and developing proposals for how their parents can improve the situation.

Meanwhile, counsellors are in their own paradoxical situation in as much as their professional ethos and training encourages them to place the child's 'story' at the heart of their work and avoid 'leading' the child or judging their words or actions. However, the general reluctance of children to produce the kinds of actions required (which derives partly from the very fact that children are thus being asked to speak in terms outside the normative parameters of child-adult interaction), means that counsellors often end up formulating the child's words in counselling-relevant terms, or proffering an assessment of their own on described circumstances in the absence of an assessment from the child.

These twin paradoxes are mutually intertwined, and they permeate the discourse of child counselling. But more than that, they enable us to account for the forms of talk and interactional strategies that previous chapters have revealed. The fact that children are both situated as children-within-the-family yet encouraged to speak in ways that are outside the normative bounds for children-in-interaction-with-adults provides grounds for their reluctance to speak in ways that 'communicate' about emotions, feelings and concerns. By the same token, counsellors' orientation to the counselling session as an environment where such 'communication' should ideally take place provides grounds for their seeking to topicalise emotions, feelings and concerns even where those are not overtly topicalised in children's own talk.

In fact, the difference alluded to here between 'talk' and 'communication' is fundamental to understanding many of the interactional practices of child counselling, and indeed of counselling and psychotherapy in general.

Child counselling and the difference between 'talking' and 'communicating'

Right at the start of the book I quoted Silverman's (1996: 208) remark that any form of counselling 'offers an institutionalised incitement to speak according to its own practical theories'. As this suggests, the forms of speech that are characteristic of counselling are different in many ways from those we might find in other arenas of social interaction. In particular, there is a specific conception of what it means to speak successfully in a counselling framework that rests on a distinction between talking (or 'just talking') and communicating.[1]

This distinction is not unique to counselling (though it may have special resonances in that context). As Cameron (2000) has described it, contemporary western culture is characterised by the increasing promulgation of the view that 'communication' is the key to solving many of the problems of everyday life. She describes various arenas of work and leisure in which the phrase 'it's good to talk' has gone from being a mere platitude to a ritually invoked standard of good citizenship. Counselling, and the associated 'talking cures' of psychoanalysis and psychotherapy, can be thought to play a central role in this incitement to communicate. Indeed, the very phrase talking cure, originally associated with early developments in psychoanalysis, has entered everyday parlance, albeit in a generally pejorative sense.

As Cameron (2000) points out, in the proliferation of handbooks, self-help books and manuals that emphasise how 'good communication' makes people better workers, citizens, parents or relationship partners, there is a key distinction between the concepts of 'talking' and 'communicating'. To communicate, in this context, means more than just to talk. Communication is prioritised as the genuine expression of feelings, as genuine care for the other, as the authentic attainment of mutual understanding in a mutually beneficial process. In other words, it is seen as an altogether 'good thing' which, though it may be an ideal, should nevertheless be constantly striven for in human interpersonal relations.

For Cameron (2000), this means that certain forms of talking—often counterintuitive and sometimes decidedly strange—are promoted as the means to achieving the goal of good communication. In counselling, there are many such forms. Take, for example, the practice of 'mirroring', advocated in certain schools of relationship mediation. Here, disputing spouses are encouraged to respond to their partner's complaints about their behaviour by, first, allowing the complaint to be stated without interruption, then 'mirroring' the complaint by repeating back their understanding of it, prefaced by the phrase 'What I hear you saying to me is . . .'.

---

1. A notion that is embodied in the very title of a doctoral thesis I supervised applying conversation analysis to psychotherapeutic discourse: 'Not Just Talking' (Pain 2003).

Here is an (invented) example:[2]

(1) Invented example of 'mirroring'
```
1    Spouse 1: All I ever get from you is criticism and negative
2              attitudes.
3    Spouse 2: What I hear you saying to me is that you feel I am
4              sometimes too negative, and maybe a bit over-
5              critical in my actions.
```

The 'mirroring' repetition (lines 3–5) is designed to discourage the early production of a defensive or argumentative reaction to the first speaker's complaint by occupying the space in which such reactions would ordinarily occur: that is, the next turn. Thus, although chains of such 'What I hear you saying'-prefaced repetitions are very different from the way that talk unfolds in ordinary conversation, they are clearly designed to have specific therapeutic effects in the context of the counselling room—for instance, to defuse potential conflict. This is an example of how an intentionally out-of-the-ordinary discourse practice is bound up with the advocation of 'good communication'—that is, achieving mutually beneficial understandings—that underpins some schools of thought in therapeutic practice.

In his work on AIDS counselling, Peräkylä (1995) describes other specialised practices such as 'circular questioning' and 'live open supervision' which are derived from the Milan School of systemic family therapy (Boscolo et al., 1986). In circular questioning, the counsellor raises 'delicate' matters concerning, for example, sexual practices or fears about the future not by asking the client directly, but by asking his or her partner to speculate openly on what they believe the client's answer might be (all this in the presence of the client). For example:

(2) From Peräkylä 1995
```
     C=Counsellor, E=Client, BF=client's boyfriend
1     C:   What are some of the things that you think E:dward might
2          have to do.=He says he doesn't know where to go from
3          here maybe: and awaiting results and things.
5          (0.6)
6→    C:   What d'you think's worrying him.
7          (0.4)
8→    BF:  Uh::m hhhhhh I think it's just fear of the unknow:n.
9→    E:   Mm[:
10    C:      [Oka:y.
```

---

2. CA generally eschews the use of invented data examples in favour of those drawn from recordings of interaction in natural settings. The reasons behind this are outlined in Chapter 2. That general analytical position, however, does not rule out occasional use of invented examples for purely illustrative purposes, as here.

Note the third person reference to 'Edward' (the client) in lines 1-3, and again in the question in line 6. After a brief pause, in line 8 the boyfriend responds with an answer that is marked as an opinion about Edward's possible worries (i.e. 'I think it's just fear of the unknow:n'). Finally, notice how Edward himself subsequently takes a brief turn to confirm that speculation (line 9) before the counsellor acknowledges the response in line 10. In Peräkylä's (1995) account, the utterance in line 9 serves as an indication that, although the circular questioning has sought to have BF speculate on the concerns of the client, the client himself works to display (by agreeing) that he is nevertheless the 'possessor' of his own thoughts.

Live open supervision, another way of topicalising delicate matters, involves two counsellors, one engaged in the primary counselling and the other ostensibly an observer. The second counsellor addresses a question to the first, but implicitly situates the client as the one best positioned to produce an answer 'by virtue of the "content" of the question concerning matters that the client is expected to know best' (Peräkylä 1995: 335). Here is one example:

(3) From Peräkylä 1995
     C1 & C2=Co-counsellors, M=Michael, the client
     1 → C2: How much does (0.2) Michael want to know
     2   about (0.8) how far he's (in[to AIDS)
     3 → M: [Well I think I should
     4   know everything.=I think it's only- only right. (Isn't
     5   it really).
     6   C1: [Mm
     7   C2: [One other question first before we go into (what he
     8 →   might be doing) is that .hhh (0.7) what if he did get
     9   AIDS,=what does he think (0.7) will be: (0.2) the
     10→   hardest thing for him.=What does he fear most.
     11   (0.8)
     12 M: I think (.) accepting it I suppose.

Note here that the question in lines 1-2 is directed towards the co-counsellor, referring to the client (Michael) in the third person. Nevertheless, Michael himself readily responds to the question, beginning his answer in line 3 in overlap with the final clause of C2's question. Later in the extract (lines 8-10) we again find questions using the third person, this time followed by a pause (line 11). Eventually, the answer is once more produced by the client even though the question was ostensibly addressed to the co-counsellor.

Both of these practices are designed as ways of making clients more aware of their own thought processes, and the impacts of their actions on others, through producing either a temporal or a grammatical distance between the delicate matter being topicalised and the client's own response to that matter. However, as Peräkylä (1995: 335) points out, such practices are also of 'particular interest because forms of indirectness that would occur relatively rarely in ordinary conversation have been conventionalised as central elements of a therapeutic technique'.

It seems, then, that rather than Silverman's (1996) phrase, 'an incitement to speak', it is more that counselling discourse is animated by an incitement to 'communicate'—that is, to speak but in a certain kind of way. For counsellors, the content of their utterances in interaction with clients indicates that such communication should ideally be about feelings, concerns and reasons.

As the preceding chapters show, in child counselling we do not tend to find speech practices as out-of-the-ordinary as those just illustrated. Like most counselling, child counselling talk is quasi-conversational in structure, with no special constraints on the type of turns taken by each participant or on their length; nor even, except in fairly subtle ways, on their content.[3] Yet within the quasi-conversational structure of child counselling the incitement to do more than 'just talk', to communicate about feelings, concerns and reasons, is readily detectable.

Thus, we have seen how counsellors routinely seek the viewpoints of children on how they feel about events associated with family separation using a version of the perspective-display series (Chapter 4) and how they seek to 'translate' children's internal feelings about such events and their consequences into interactionally available therapeutic objects using the practice of formulation (Chapter 5). Counsellors also have been seen to try getting children to explain or provide reasons for why their life situation is the way it is. In general, throughout the analysis, one major question has been that of how counsellors bring to the surface the concerns that children might have about their problematic family situation. As we have seen, children rarely volunteer information on their worries or concerns. Nevertheless counsellors seem to be working on the assumption that such worries or concerns indeed exist. Counsellors therefore construct interpretations of the child's talk or other activities that favour the possibility that the child may be 'angry', 'confused', 'upset' and so forth.

In such ways the incitement to communicate (about feelings, concerns and reasons) clearly operates in child counselling. A major factor here is the practice of 'active listening', which in counselling studies refers to the ways in which counsellors seek to show responsivity and empathy towards what the child is saying. However, through our examination of naturally-occurring child counselling talk, we have seen that this practice is more complex than texts on counselling have

---

3. Indeed, outside of the theoretically-driven practices of live open supervision and circular questioning, the same can be said about a large proportion of Peräkylä's (1995) AIDS counselling data.

acknowledged. Specifically, conversation analysis reveals how the practices of active listening are bound up in the construction of the child as an object of therapy. Active listening is therefore involved not just in responding empathically to what the child says, but in interpreting and reconstructing what the child says so that it can be made relevant to the agendas of counselling. In other words, it is an integral part of what I referred to in previous chapters as counsellors' therapeutic vision.

'Therapeutic vision' and the power dynamic in child counselling

Therapeutic vision is a specific type of a more general phenomenon that Goodwin (1994) calls 'professional vision'. This is a way of seeing and understanding events according to occupationally-relevant norms. For instance, on first looking at a sample through a microscope a novice molecular biologist may see an array of splodges, but following training and inculcation in the professional knowledge of molecular biology, he or she will be able to exercise professional vision to see a particular cellular structure.

For Goodwin (1994) the socially organised practices of professional vision involve 'highlighting' certain features of a perceptual field; 'coding' those features according to given knowledge schemas; and often producing material representations (such as diagrams, graphs, tables or models) of the salient phenomena. Goodwin (1994) analyses this in the discourse of geologists and in the context of legal argumentation. However, there are similarities in the practices of therapeutic vision as revealed in the preceding chapters.

For example, child counsellors routinely seek to 'highlight' those aspects of children's talk that can be heard to be relevant for family-related or feelings-related matters. The interpretations they produce and offer to the child in perspective-display and question-answer-formulation sequences can also be seen as 'coding' events according to counselling-relevant schemas. In previous chapters I have referred to these as counselling tropes: they include what seem to be standard messages such as 'parents should sort it out'; 'it is not the child's fault'; 'children often get caught in the middle of parents' fights'; and 'parents' fights can make children feel angry/sad/guilty'.

The success of therapeutic vision, in seeking to bring into play counselling-relevant topics and interpretations, depends in part on children's recognition of, and willingness to go along with, that aim. The data, however, reveal wide variability in children's agreement to engage in counselling-relevant talk. We have examined some key resistance strategies adopted by children, and analysed the strategies and techniques brought into play by counsellors in response. In particular, in Chapter 6, the use of 'I don't know' in response to counsellors' questions was investigated as a way of acting strategically and attempting to exercise some form of power over the ways that counselling-relevant agendas are pursued in questions.

Child counselling sessions can therefore be seen as arenas of social action in which not only are different interactional competencies being deployed by counsellors as well as by children, but also a power dynamic threads in and out of the discourse. By that, I do not mean to refer to any large-scale exercise of oppression: it is not that counsellors are to be seen as subjugating children against their will, for example. Rather, it is to draw attention to the ways in which counsellors and children, in conducting interaction according to what they understand to be the distinctive requirements of the setting, also become engaged in a micro-level network of power and resistance.

Power is an issue on which conversation analysts have tended to remain agnostic (Hutchby 1999). Schegloff (1991) argues that the more analysis focuses on sociological variables such as power, the less it tends to focus on the actual practices of talk-in-interaction, and the greater the tendency towards a reification of power. While not denying the existence of power, Schegloff's recommendation is that analysis should be restricted as far as possible to explicating the practices, without setting any a priori questions about the features of interaction, whether institutional or mundane, that one is going to analyse. The implication here seems to be that analysts should only have recourse to concepts such as power once they are forced to do so by virtue of some otherwise unexplainable interactional phenomenon.

One upshot of this is that it leaves CA open to the kind of critique offered by politically-oriented discourse analysts such as Fairclough (1995: 23), who believes that conversation analysis is 'resistant to linking properties of talk with higher-level features of society and culture—relations of power, ideologies, cultural values.' To some, of course, this simply begs the question of how we are to show such linkages without assuming their existence a priori. However, I take the view that Fairclough's remark reflects a common, though inaccurate, conception of the kind of work that CA produces.

As myself and others have argued before (Davis 1988; Hutchby 1996, 1999; Watson 1990), while CA is not in favour of the view that power relations somehow preexist and determine the course of actual concrete encounters, by focusing on the local management of talk-in-interaction it can in fact provide compelling accounts of how power comes to operate as a feature of, and is used as a resource in, institutional interaction. The crucial factor to be borne in mind, in line with Schegloff's (1991) account, is that power cannot be read off as a feature of objectively-existing relationships between participants. Rather, power 'must be firmly located in the systematic examination of features integral to the discourse itself' (Watson 1990: 280).

Many CA accounts of institutional discourse (some of them discussed in Chapter 2) focus on the existence of asymmetries without going on to make explicit claims about power. But that is not to say that those kinds of claims cannot be made. By showing how participants display an orientation to institutional settings by engaging in certain activities and refraining from others, and illustrating how activities such as questioning are used to constrain the options of a coparticipant, CA can also be used to demonstrate how power can be a feature of those activities. What is implied by these studies is that oriented-to activity patterns, such as differences in questioning and answering, proferring and resisting topics, may themselves be intrinsic to the play of power in institutional interactions.

Foucault (1977) argued that power is not something that is possessed by one agent or collectivity and lacked by another, but a potential that has to be instantiated within a network equally including those who exercise power and those who accept or resist it. The network itself should be viewed as a structure of possibilities, and not as a concrete relationship between determinate social entities. Against the tendency to conceive of power only as a 'big' phenomenon, operating at the largest scale within social formations, Foucault (1977) suggested that power is pervasive even at the smallest level of interpersonal relationships.

The CA approach adopted in this book encourages us to view power in a similar way: not as a zero-sum game but as a set of potentials which, while always present, can be variably exercised, resisted, shifted around and struggled over by social agents. Thus, as counsellors seek to exercise therapeutic vision, to frame children's utterances and other actions in terms of key child counselling tropes, and to encourage children to cooperate in the topicalisation of these tropes, they can be seen to be instantiating the incitement to communicate, which in turn is a form of discursive power. But while counsellors may be involved in promoting the institutionalised incitement to communicate, children are equally involved in accepting or resisting that incitement. And while children may thus be conceived as exercising their own forms of discursive power (the power to decline a response, to initiate a different topic, and so forth), counsellors are equally involved in accepting or resisting those tactics.

In conclusion: The importance of fine-grained observation

The key point in all this is that the phenomena summarised above, and described in detail in the previous chapters, only become observable by means of the conversation analytic approach with its insistence on the empirical analysis of naturally-occurring interaction. This leads us, finally, to some of the implications of the book for counselling practitioners themselves.

Hopefully, what these chapters offer is a novel perspective on counsellors' own understanding of therapy as a process; on what can be understood as successful counselling; and on the process of therapeutic change. Challenging the conventional view of counselling as a reasoned process directed towards the achievement of specifiable 'outcomes', the book reveals counselling talk as a largely contingent and pragmatic enterprise, in which counsellors skilfully engage in constructing the child as a therapeutic subject using whatever discursive resources are at hand.

Counselling, as Silverman (1996) remarks, is often conceived both by its practitioners and the lay public as an 'enabling' discourse. Yet any enablement that gets done is unavoidably accomplished amid the contingencies of unfolding talk-in-interaction. This means that counsellors must deal, in a practical and real-time fashion, with the verbal and non-verbal actions and reactions of clients. At various points in this book we have seen that these contingencies lead to forms and patterns of interaction that are significantly beyond the guidelines and recommendations typically found in child counselling manuals. Thus, as Silverman (1996: 209) aptly puts it, 'while power and resistance may be ubiquitous in everyday life, their concrete form and practical implications are locally contingent matters that cannot be fully anticipated by looking only at the formal strategies of the professional literature.'

Textbooks and manuals aimed at child counselling practitioners typically extol the virtues of certain counselling techniques, instruct the counsellor on the importance of placing the child's 'story' at the heart of what they do, define key moments in the 'cycle of therapeutic change' that counselling is designed to inculcate, and offer definitions and guidelines on the kinds of activities that might be involved in enabling this. However, there is rarely any evidence that such definitions and guidelines are based on detailed empirical observation of naturally occurring child counselling discourse. Whatever information might be offered by such handbooks, therefore, it is important to carry out fine-grained observational analyses of talk-in-interaction in the course of naturally-occurring counselling sessions. Only by doing this can we understand the true richness of the interactional resources brought into play by both counsellors and children in the management of therapeutic interaction as it unfolds.

References

Alderson, P. 1993. *Children's Consent to Surgery*. Buckingham: Open University Press.
Archard, R. 1993. *Children: Rights and childhood*. London: Routledge.
Arminen, I. 2005. *Institutional Interaction: Studies of talk at work*. Aldershot: Ashgate.
Aronsson, K. and Cederborg, A-C. 1996. Coming of age in family therapy talk: Perspective setting in multiparty problem formulations. *Discourse Processes* 21: 191–212.
Atkinson, J. M. 1984. *Our Masters' Voices: The language and body language of politics*. London: Methuen.
Atkinson, J. M. and Drew, P. 1979. *Order in Court: The organisation of verbal interaction in judicial settings*. London: Macmillan.
Baker, C. 1982. Adolescent-adult talk as a practical interpretive problem. In G. Payne and E. Cuff (eds), *Doing Teaching: The practical management of classrooms*. London: Batsford.
Baker, C. 1984. The search for adultness: Membership work in adolescent-adult talk. *Human Studies* 7: 301–23.
Bateson, G. 1956. The message 'This is play'. In B. Schaffner (ed.), *Group Processes: Transactions of the second conference*, 145–242. New York NY: Josiah Macy Jr. Foundation.
Bateson, G. and Mead, M. 1942. *Balinese Character: A photographic analysis*. New York NY: New York Academy of Sciences.
Birdwhistell, R. 1952. *Introduction to Kinesics: An annotation system for the analysis of body motion and gesture*. Washington DC: Foreign Services Institute, US Department of State.
Bergmann, J. 1992. Veiled morality: Notes on discretion in psychiatry. In P. Drew and J. Heritage (eds), *Talk at Work*. Cambridge: Cambridge University Press.
Blaxter, L., Hughes, C. and Tight, M. 1996. *How to Research*. Buckingham: Open University Press.
Boscolo, L. Cecchin, G., Hoffman, L. and Penn, P. 1986. *Milan Systemic Family Therapy: Conversations in theory and practice*. New York NY: Basic Books.
Bruner, J. 1986. *Actual Minds, Possible Worlds*. Cambridge MA: Harvard University Press.
Bryman, A. 1988. *Quantity and Quality in Social Research*. London: Routledge.
Cameron, D. 2000. *Good to Talk?* London: Sage.
Chapman, M. 1988. Contextuality and directionality of cognitive development. *Human Development* 31: 92–106.
Clayman, S. 1988. Displaying neutrality in television news interviews. *Social Problems* 35: 474–92.
Clayman, S. 1992. Footing in the achievement of neutrality: The case of news interview discourse. In P. Drew and J. Heritage (eds.), *Talk At Work*. Cambridge: Cambridge University Press.
Clayman, S. and Heritage, J. 2004. *The News Interview*. Cambridge: Cambridge University Press.
Coulter, J. 1982. Remarks on the conceptualization of social structure. *Philosophy of the Social Sciences* 12: 33–46.

Danby, S. and Baker, C. 1998. 'What's the problem?' Restoring social order in the preschool classroom. In I. Hutchby and J. Moran-Ellis (eds), *Children and Social Competence: Arenas of action*. London: Falmer Press.

Davidson, J. 1984. Subsequent versions of invitations, offers, requests, and proposals dealing with potential or actual rejection. In J. M. Atkinson and J. C. Heritage (eds), *Structures of Social Action: Studies in conversation analysis*. Cambridge: Cambridge University Press.

Davis, K. 1988. *Power Under the Microscope*. Dordrecht: Foris.

Drew, P. 1989. Recalling someone from the past. In D. Roger and P. Bull (eds), *Conversation*. Clevedon: Multilingual Matters.

Drew, P. 1992. Contested evidence in courtroom cross-examination: The case of a trial for rape. In P. Drew and J. Heritage (eds), *Talk at Work*. Cambridge: Cambridge University Press.

Drew, P. and Heritage, J. 1992. Introduction: Analysing talk at work. In P. Drew and J. Heritage (eds), *Talk at Work*. Cambridge: Cambridge University Press.

Eder, D. 1991. Serious and playful disputes: Variation in conflict talk among female adolescents. In A. Grimshaw (ed.), *Conflict Talk*. Cambridge: Cambridge University Press.

Erickson, F. 2004. *Talk and Social Theory*. Cambridge: Polity.

Ervin-Tripp, S. and Mitchell-Kernan, C. (eds). 1977. *Child Discourse*. New York NY: Academic Press.

Evans-Pritchard, E. 1936. *Witchcraft, Oracles and Magic among the Azande*. Oxford: Oxford University Press.

Fairclough, N. 1995. *Media Discourse*. London: Edward Arnold.

Fielding, N. 1993. Ethnography. In N. Gilbert (ed.), *Researching Social Life*. London: Sage.

Foddy, W. 1993. *Constructing Questions for Interviews and Questionnaires: Theory and practice in social research*. Cambridge: Cambridge University Press.

Foucault, M. 1977. *Power/Knowledge*. Hemel Hempstead: Harvester.

Fowler, F. J. and Mangione, T. W. 1990. *Standardised Survey Interviewing: Minimising interviewer-related error* [Applied Social Research Methods Series 18]. London: Sage.

Frankel, R. 1984. From sentence to sequence: Understanding the medical encounter through microinteractional analysis. *Discourse Processes* 7: 135–70.

Frankel, R. 1990. Talking in interviews: A dispreference for patient-initiated questions in physician-patient encounters. In G. Psathas (ed.), *Interaction Competence*. Washington DC: University Press of America.

Garfinkel, H. 1967. *Studies in Ethnomethodology*. Englewood Cliffs NJ: Prentice-Hall.

Garfinkel, H. and Sacks, H. 1970. On formal structures of practical actions. In J. C. McKinney and E. A. Teryakian (eds), *Theoretical Sociology*. New York NY: Appleton-Century-Crofts.

Garvey, C. 1984. *Children's Talk*. Cambridge MA: Harvard University Press.

Geldard, K. and Geldard, D. 1997. *Counselling Children: A practical introduction*. London: Sage.

Gilligan, C. 1982. *In a Different Voice: Psychological theory and women's development*. Cambridge MA: Harvard University Press.

Goffman, E. 1959. *The Presentation of Self in Everyday Life*. New York NY: Doubleday.

Goffman, E. 1961. *Encounters*. New York NY: Bobbs-Merrill.

Goffman, E. 1981. *Forms of Talk*. Oxford: Blackwell.

Goode, D. 1991. Kids, culture and innocents. In F. Waksler (ed.), *Studying the Social Worlds of Children*. London: Falmer Press.

Goodwin, C. 1994. Professional vision. *American Anthropologist* 96: 606–33.

Goodwin, M. H. 1990. *He-Said-She-Said: Talk as social organisation among black children*. Bloomington IN: Indiana University Press.

Greatbatch, D. 1988. A turn-taking system for British news interviews. *Language in Society* 17: 401–30.
Hammersley, M. 1992. *What's Wrong with Ethnography? Methodological explorations.* London: Routledge.
Hammersley, M. and Atkinson, P. 1983. *Ethnography: Principles in practice.* London: Routledge.
Hammersley, M. and Atkinson, P. 1995. *Ethnography: Principles in practice, second edition.* London: Routledge.
Hardman, C. 1973. Can there be an anthropology of childhood? *Journal of the Anthropological Society of Oxford* 4: 85–99.
Heath, C. 1992. The delivery and reception of diagnosis in the general practice consultation. In P. Drew and J. Heritage (eds), *Talk At Work: Interaction in institutional settings.* Cambridge: Cambridge University Press.
Heritage, J. 1984. A change-of-state token and aspects of its sequential placement. In J. M. Atkinson and J. Heritage (eds.), *Structures of Social Action: Studies in conversation analysis.* Cambridge: Cambridge University Press.
Heritage, J. 1985. Analysing news interviews: Aspects of the production of talk for an overhearing audience. In T.A. van Dijk (ed.), *Handbook of Discourse Analysis,* Vol. 3: *Discourse and dialogue.* London: Academic Press.
Heritage, J. 1989. Current developments in conversation analysis. In D. Roger and P. Bull (eds.), *Conversation.* Clevedon: Multilingual Matters.
Heritage, J. and Atkinson, J. M. 1984. Introduction. In J. M. Atkinson and J. Heritage (eds.), *Structures of Social Action: Studies in conversation analysis.* Cambridge: Cambridge University Press.
Heritage, J. and Greatbatch, D. 1991. On the institutional character of institutional talk: The case of news interviews. In D. Boden and D. Zimmerman (eds.), *Talk and Social Structure.* Cambridge: Polity Press.
Heritage, J. and Sefi, S. 1992. Dilemmas of advice: Aspects of the delivery and reception of advice in interactions between Health Visitors and first-time mothers. In P. Drew and J. Heritage (eds.), *Talk At Work: Interaction in institutional settings.* Cambridge: Cambridge University Press.
Heritage, J. and Watson, D.R. 1979. Formulations as conversational objects. In G. Psathas (ed.), *Everyday Language.* Mahwah NJ: Lawrence Erlbaum Associates.
Hopper, R. 1992. *Telephone Conversation.* Indiana IN: Indiana University Press.
Hutchby, I. 1996 *Confrontation Talk: Arguments, asymmetries and power on talk radio.* Mahwah NJ: Lawrence Erlbaum Associates.
Hutchby, I. 1999. Beyond agnosticism: Conversation analysis and the sociological agenda. *Research on Language and Social Interaction* 32: 85–93.
Hutchby, I. 2001. *Conversation and Technology: From the telephone to the internet.* Cambridge: Polity Press.
Hutchby, I. 2006. *Media Talk: Conversation analysis and the study of broadcasting.* Maidenhead: Open University Press.
Hutchby, I. and Moran-Ellis, J. (eds). 1998. *Children and Social Competence: Arenas of action.* London: Falmer Press.
Hutchby, I. and Wooffitt, R. 1998. *Conversation Analysis.* Cambridge: Polity Press.
James, A. 1993. *Childhood Identities: Social Relationships and the Self in Children's Experiences.* Edinburgh: Edinburgh University Press.

James, A. and Prout, A. (eds). 1990. *Constructing and Reconstructing Childhood: Contemporary issues in the sociological study of childhood*. London: Falmer Press.
Jefferson, G. 1980. On 'trouble-premonitory' response to inquiry. *Sociological Inquiry* 50: 153–85.
Jefferson, G. 1986. Notes on latency in overlap onset. *Human Studies* 9: 153–83.
Judd, C. M., Smith, E. R. and Kidder, L. H. 1991. *Research Methods in Social Relations: Sixth edition*. London: Harcourt Brace Jovanovich College Publishers.
Kendon, A. 1982. The organisation of behaviour in face-to-face interaction: Observations on the development of a methodology. In K. R. Scherer and P. Ekman (eds), *Handbook of Methods in Nonverbal Behaviour Research*. Cambridge: Cambridge University Press.
Kendon, A. 1990. *Conducting Interaction*. Cambridge: Cambridge University Press.
Labov, W. 1972. *Language in the Inner City*. Philadelphia PA: University of Pennsylvania Press.
Lein, L. and Brenneis, D. 1978. Children's disputes in three speech communities. *Language in Society* 7: 299–323.
Levinson, S. 1983. *Pragmatics*. Cambridge: Cambridge University Press.
Lynch, M. 2003. From naturally-occurring data to naturally organised ordinary activites: Comment on Speer. *Discourse Studies* 4: 531–8.
McHoul, A. 1978. The organisation of turns at formal talk in the classroom. *Language in Society* 19: 183–213.
McQuown, N. (ed.). 1971. *The Natural History of an Interview* [Microfilm Collection of Manuscripts on Cultural Anthropology, 15th Series]. Chicago IL: University of Chicago, Joseph Regenstein Library, Department of Photoduplication.
MacIntyre, A. 1970a. Is understanding religion compatible with believing? In B. Turner (ed.), *Rationality*. Oxford: Blackwell.
MacIntyre, A. 1970b. The idea of a social science. In B. Turner (ed.), *Rationality*. Oxford: Blackwell.
Mackay, R. 1973. Conceptions of children and models of socialisation. In H. P. Dreitzel (ed.), *Childhood and Socialisation*. London: Collier-Macmillan.
Mandell, N. 1991. The least-adult role in studying children. In F. C. Waksler (ed.), *Studying the Social Worlds of Children*. London: Falmer Press.
Marlaire, C. and Maynard, D. 1990. Standardised testing as an interactional phenomenon. *Sociology of Education* 63: 83–101.
Mayall, B. (ed.). 1994a. *Children's Childhoods Observed and Experienced*. London: Falmer Press.
Mayall, B. 1994b. Children in action at home and in school. In B. Mayall (ed.), *Children's Childhoods Observed and Experienced*. London: Falmer Press.
Maykut, P. and Morehouse, R. 1994. *Beginning Qualitative Research: A philosophic and practical guide*. London: Falmer Press.
Maynard, D.W. 1985. How children start arguments. *Language in Society* 14: 1–30.
Maynard, D.W. 1986. The development of argumentative skills among children. In A. Adler and P. Adler (eds), *Sociological Studies of Child Development*, Vol. 1. Greenwich CT: JAI Press.
Maynard, D. 1989. Perspective-display sequences in conversation. *Western Journal of Speech Communication* 53: 91–113.
Maynard, D. 1991. Interaction and asymmetry in clinical discourse. *American Journal of Sociology* 97: 448–95.
Mehan, H. 1979. *Learning Lessons: Social organisation in the classroom*. Cambridge MA: Harvard University Press.

Michels, B. and Prince A. 1992. *The Children Act and Medical Practice*. Bristol: Jordan and Sons.
Ochs, E. 1979. Transcription as theory. In E. Ochs and B. Schieffelin (eds), *Developmental Pragmatics*. London: Academic Press.
Ochs, E. 1988. *Culture and Language Development*. Cambridge: Cambridge University Press.
Ochs, E. and Schieffelin, B. 1979. *Developmental Pragmatics*. London: Academic Press.
Ochs, E. and Schieffelin, B. 1983. *Acquiring Conversational Competence*. London: Routledge.
Pain, J. 2003. Not Just Talking: A sociological study of the organisation of dialogue in one-to-one psychotherapy. PhD dissertation, Brunel University.
Parsons, T. 1951. *The Social System*. New York NY: Free Press.
Peräkylä, A. 1995. *AIDS Counselling: Institutional interaction and clinical practice*. Cambridge: Cambridge University Press.
Piaget, J. 1926. *The Language and Thought of the Child*. London: Kegan, Paul, Trench, Trubner and Co.
Pomerantz, A. 1984. Agreeing and disagreeing with assessments: Some features of preferred/dispreferred turn-shapes. In J. M. Atkinson and J. Heritage (eds), *Structures of Social Action: Studies in conversation analysis*. Cambridge: Cambridge University Press.
Potter, J. 1996a. Discourse analysis and constructionist approaches: Theoretical background. In J. T. E. Richardson (ed.), *Handbook of Qualitative Research Methods for Psychology and the Social Sciences*. Leicester: B. P. S. Books.
Potter, J. 1996b. *Representing Reality: Discourse, rhetoric and social construction*. London: Sage.
Potter, J. 2003. Two kinds of natural. *Discourse Studies* 4: 539–42.
Prout, A. and James, A. 1990. A new paradigm for the sociology of childhood? Provenance, promise and problems. In A. James and A. Prout (eds), *Constructing and Reconstructing Childhood*. London: Falmer Press.
Puchta, C. and Potter, J. 1999. Asking elaborate questions: Focus groups and the management of spontaneity. *Journal of Sociolinguistics* 3: 314–35.
Qvortrup, J. 1990. A voice for children in statistical and social accounting: A plea for children's rights to be heard. In A. James and A. Prout (eds), *Constructing and Reconstructing Childhood*. London: Falmer Press.
Qvortrup, J. 1994. Childhood matters: An introduction. In J. Qvortrup, M. Bardy, G. Sgritta and H. Wintersberger (eds), *Childhood Matters: Social theory, practice and politics*. Aldershot: Avebury.
Robson, C. 1993. *Real World Research: A resource for social scientists and practioner-researchers*. Oxford: Blackwell.
Sacks, H. 1972. On the analysability of stories by children. In J. Gumperz and D. Hymes (eds), *Directions in Sociolinguistics*. New York NY: Holt, Rinehart and Winston.
Sacks, H. 1984. Notes on methodology. In J. M. Atkinson and J. Heritage (eds) *Structures of Social Action: Studies in conversation analysis*. Cambridge: Cambridge University Press.
Sacks, H. 1975. Everyone has to lie. In B. Blount and M. Sanchez (eds), *Sociocultural Dimensions of Language Use*. New York NY: Academic Press.
Sacks, H. 1987. On the preferences for agreement and contiguity in sequences in conversation. In G. Button and J. R. E. Lee (eds), *Talk and Social Organisation*. Clevedon: Multilingual Matters.
Sacks, H. 1992. *Lectures on Conversation*, Vol. 1 & Vol. 2. Oxford: Blackwell.
Sacks, H., Schegloff, E. A. and Jefferson, G. 1974. A simplest systematics for the organisation of turn-taking for conversation. *Language* 50: 696–735.

Schegloff, E. A. 1982 Discourse as an interactional achievement: some uses of 'uh huh' and other things that come between sentences. In D. Tannen (ed.), *Analysing Discourse: Text and talk*. Washington DC: Georgetown University Press.

Schegloff, E. A. 1984. On some questions and ambiguities in conversation. In J. M. Atkinson and J. Heritage (eds), *Structures of Social Action: Studies in conversation analysis*. Cambridge: Cambridge University Press.

Schegloff, E. A. 1991. Reflections on talk and social structure. In D. Boden and D. Zimmerman (eds), *Talk and Social Structure*. Cambridge: Polity Press.

Schegloff, E. A. and Sacks, H. 1973. Opening up closings. *Semiotica* 7: 289–327.

Schieffelin, B. 1990. *The Give and Take of Everyday Life*. Cambridge: Cambridge University Press.

Sharpe, S. and Cowie, H. 1998. *Counselling and Supporting Children in Distress*. London: Sage.

Sheldon, A. 1992a. Conflict talk: Sociolinguistic challenges to self-assertion and how young girls meet them. *Merrill-Palmer Quarterly* 38: 95–117.

Sheldon, A. 1992b. Preschool girls' discourse competence: Managing conflict. In K. Hall, M. Bucholtz and B. Moonwomon (eds), *Locating Power*. Berkeley CA: Berkeley Linguistic Society.

Sheldon, A. 1996. You can be the baby brother but you aren't born yet: Preschool girls' negotiation for power and access in pretend play. *Research on Language and Social Interaction* 29: 57–80.

Silverman, D. 1983. The clinical subject: Adolescents in a cleft-palate clinic. *Sociology of Health and Illness* 5: 253–74.

Silverman, D. 1987. *Communication and Medical Practice*. London: Sage.

Silverman, D. 1996. *Discourses of Counselling*, London: Sage.

Silverman, D. Baker, C. and Keogh, J. 1998. The case of the silent child: Advice-giving and advice-reception in the parent-teacher interview. In I. Hutchby and J. Moran-Ellis (eds), *Children and Social Competence: Arenas of action*. London: Falmer Press.

Speer, S.A. 2003a. 'Natural' and 'contrived' data: A sustainable distinction? *Discourse Studies* 4: 511–26.

Speer, S.A. 2003b. Transcending the 'natural'/'contrived' distinction: A rejoinder to ten Have, Lynch and Potter. *Discourse Studies* 4: 543–8.

Speer, S.A. and Hutchby, I. 2003. From ethics to analytics: Aspects of participants' orientations to the presence and relevance of recording devices. *Sociology* 37: 315–37.

Stubbs, M. 1983. *Discourse Analysis: The sociolinguistic analysis of natural language*. Oxford: Basil Blackwell.

Suchman, L. and Jordan, B. 1990. Interactional troubles in face-to-face survey interviews. *Journal of the American Statistical Association* 85: 232–41.

Ten Have, P. 1999. *Doing Conversation Analysis: A practical guide*. London: Sage.

Ten Have, P. 2003. Ontology or methodology? Comments on Speer's 'Natural' and 'contrived' data: A sustainable distinction? *Discourse Studies* 4: 527–30.

Thornborrow, J. 1998. Children's participation in the discourse of children's television. In I. Hutchby and J. Moran-Ellis (eds), *Children and Social Competence: Arenas of action*. London: Falmer Press.

Thorne, B. 1993. *Gender Play*. Buckingham: Open University Press.

Vygotsky, L. 1978. *Mind in Society*. Cambridge MA: Harvard University Press.

Waksler, F. C. (ed.). 1991. *Studying the Social Worlds of Children*. London: Falmer Press.

Watson, D.R. 1990. Some features of the elicitation of confessions in murder interrogations. In G. Psathas (ed.), *Interaction Competence*. Washington DC: University Press of America.
Winch, P. 1970a. The idea of a social science. In B. Turner (ed.), *Rationality*. Oxford: Blackwell.
Winch, P. 1970b. Understanding a primitive society. In B. Turner (ed.), *Rationality*. Oxford: Blackwell.
Woolfe, R. and Dryden, W. (eds). 1996. *Handbook of Counselling Psychology*. London: Sage.

Index

A
active listening 79–82, 98, 130–1
adjacency pair 27–30
affordances 48, 57
Alderson, Patricia 14, 16
arenas of action 13–17
Arminen, Ilkka 19, 32
Aronsson, Karin 95
Atkinson, J. Maxwell 4, 20, 32, 33, 43, 44
Atkinson, Paul 42

B
Baker, Carolyn 12, 13, 102
Bateson, Gregory 19
Birdwhistell, Ray 19
Bergmann, Jörg 34
bricolage 17, 34–7, 125
Brenneis, Donald 108
British Psychological Society 41
British Sociological Association 41
Bruner, Jerome 6
Bryman, Alan 42

C
Cameron, Deborah 127
category-bound activities 86–7
childhood, sociology of 5–9
Children Act (1989), The 5
child's perspective 4, 7–9, 74, 77, 126
children's talk, sociolinguistics of 9–13
circular questioning 128–30
Clayman, Steven 32
'communicating', 127–31; see also incitement to speak
competence paradigm 5–7
conditional relevance 27
confidentiality 1, 2, 39, 40
consent 1, 3–4, 14; see also informed consent
conversation analysis 3, 4, 10, 11, 19–37, 124–6
 history of 19–20
 and naturally-occurring data 19, 20–2, 43–5
 principles of 22–30
 theory of context 31–2
Coulter, Jeff 33
counselling process 1–2

child counselling tropes 77, 88, 89, 93, 94, 112, 121, 131, 133
Cowie, Helen 80, 81

D
Danby, Susan 12
Davidson, Judy 30
Davis, Kathy 132
deflection 101; see also resistance
delicate topics 59–60, 63, 74, 78
development 5, 6–7
 and children's language 10, 63–5
 and children's competence 14
developmental psychology 5, 6, 7, 9
divorce 1, 16, 40, 41, 111, 121, 123
Drew, Paul 4, 16, 19, 20, 31, 32, 33, 34–5, 44, 45, 83, 103, 104–5
Dryden, Windy 56, 124

E
Eder, Donna 10
Ervin-Tripp, Susan 11
ethics 41, 42, 45, 56
ethnography 7, 8, 9, 10, 14, 19, 21
ethnomethodology 3, 19, 31
Evans-Pritchard, Edward 8

F
Fairclough, Norman 132
family therapy 2
feelings-talk 59, 79, 83, 90, 93, 94, 97, 99
Fielding, Nigel 42
formulations 82–90, 94, 99, 123, 131
 and resistance 94–8
 see also reformulation
Foucault, Michel 133
Frankel, Richard 35

G
Garfinkel, Harold 3, 19, 31, 82
Garvey, Catherine 10
Geldard, Kathryn 34, 37, 46,

75, 80, 81, 82, 92, 101, 102, 119, 121
Geldard, David 34, 37, 46, 75, 80, 81, 82, 92, 101, 102, 119, 121
Goffman, Erving 15, 19, 34
Goode, David 8
Goodwin, Charles 131
Goodwin, Marjorie 11, 21
Greatbatch, David 20, 31, 32, 33, 34

H
Hammersley, Martyn 42
Hardman, Charlotte 6
Heath, Christian 32, 33, 35, 36
Heritage, John 4, 16, 19, 20, 26, 30–1, 32, 33, 34, 43, 44, 82, 83, 88, 89, 91, 101
HIV/AIDS counselling 3, 35, 36, 59, 101, 128–9
Hopper, Robert 21
Hutchby, Ian 4, 20, 32, 42, 44, 57, 125, 132

I
'I don't know'
 as an avoidance strategy 104–5
 as a state of mind 116–20
 cognitive vs interactional approaches to 103–6
 playful vs. serious interpretations of 113–16
incitement to speak 3, 101, 117, 120, 127
 and incitement to 'communicate' 130, 133
informed consent 39, 40, 41, 42, 44, 45; see also consent
institutional interaction 30–7
 formal and non-formal types of 33–4

J
James, Allison 5, 7, 9, 14, 125
Jefferson, Gail 20, 24, 26, 60, 79
Jordan, Brigitte 81

K
Kendon, Adam 21
Keogh, Jayne 12, 13, 102

L
Labov, William 42
least-adult role 7–8
Lein, Laura 108
Levinson, Steven 28
live open supervision 128–30
Lynch, Michael 20

M
McHoul, Alec 11, 32
MacIntyre, Alasdair 8
Mackay, Robert 5
Mandell, Nancy 7, 8
Mayall, Berry 5, 11, 16
Maynard, Douglas 10, 60, 61, 62, 63, 74, 75, 94
Mead, Margaret 19
Mehan, Hugh 4, 20
Mitchels, Barbara 16
Milan School of Family Systems theory 2, 128
mirroring 127–8
Mitchell-Kernan, Claudia 11
Moran-Ellis, Jo 5, 125

N
newsmarkers 88, 89, 91–4

O
Ochs, Elinor 10, 21
one-way mirror dilemma 42–5
overlapping talk 24–5, 106–8

P
Pain, Jean 59, 127
participant observation 7, 8, 9, 42
Parsons, Talcott 6
peer group interaction 9, 11–12
Peräkylä, Anssi 3, 35, 36, 59, 60, 81, 101, 128, 129, 130
perspective-display series
  in conversation 61–2, 75
  in pediatric interviews 63–5, 75
  in child counselling 63–74, 76–7
Piaget, Jean 5, 6
preference 29–30
Prince, Alister 16
professional vision 131; *see also* therapeutic vision
Prout, Alan 5, 7, 9, 14, 125
Pomerantz, Anita 29, 61
Potter, Jonathan 20, 44, 81, 103, 104, 105
power 131–3

Q
QAF (question–answer–formulation) sequence 83–4
questions, discouragement of 34, 82
Qvortrup, Jens 7, 14

R
reflecting 80–1; *see also* formulations
reformulation 83; *see also* formulations
resistance 101–2, 120

S
Sacks, Harvey 3, 19, 20, 23, 24, 25, 29, 31, 33, 43, 79, 87, 102
Schegloff, Emanuel 20, 24, 31, 79, 92, 102, 132
Schieffelin, Bambi 10
Sefi, Sue 34, 101
Sharpe, Sue 80, 81
Sheldon, Amy 10
Silverman, David 3, 11, 12, 13, 56, 81, 101, 102, 124, 127, 134
social competence (of children), 9–13, 13–15; *see also* competence paradigm
socialisation 5–7
Speer, Susan 20, 42, 44
Stubbs, Michael 42
Suchman, Lucy 81
summarising 80–1; *see also* formulations
tape-recording
  and the data collection process 3–4, 39–41
  as data 19, 20, 21
  participants' orientations to 46–57
  transcription of, ix–x 20–3
  video 21, 44–5
Ten Have, Paul 20
therapeutic vision 74–7; *see also* professional vision
Thornborrow, Joanna 11
Thorne, Barrie 6, 7
turn-taking 22–30
  turn-constructional units 24
  transition-relevance places 24
  turn-type pre-allocation 33
twin paradoxes of child counselling 126

U
United Nations Charter on the Rights of the Child 5

V
videotape recording, *see* tape-recording
Vygotsky, Lev 6

W
Waksler, Frances 5, 7
Watson, Rod 82, 89, 132
Winch, Peter 8
Wooffitt, Robin 4, 20, 44
Woolfe, Ray 56, 124

In the series IMPACT: *Studies in language and society* the following titles have been published thus far or are scheduled for publication:

22 POTOWSKI, Kim and Richard CAMERON (eds.): Spanish in Contact. Policy, Social and Linguistic Inquiries. *Expected July 2007*
21 HUTCHBY, Ian: The Discourse of Child Counselling. 2007. xii, 144 pp.
20 FENYVESI, Anna (ed.): Hungarian Language Contact Outside Hungary. Studies on Hungarian as a minority language. 2005. xxii, 425 pp.
19 DEUMERT, Ana: Language Standardization and Language Change. The dynamics of Cape Dutch. 2004. xx, 362 pp.
18 DEUMERT, Ana and Wim VANDENBUSSCHE (eds.): Germanic Standardizations. Past to Present. 2003. vi, 480 pp.
17 TRINCH, Shonna L.: Latinas' Narratives of Domestic Abuse. Discrepant versions of violence. 2003. x, 315 pp.
16 BRITAIN, David and Jenny CHESHIRE (eds.): Social Dialectology. In honour of Peter Trudgill. 2003. x, 344 pp.
15 BOXER, Diana: Applying Sociolinguistics. Domains and face-to-face interaction. 2002. xii, 245 pp.
14 WEBB, Victor: Language in South Africa. The role of language in national transformation, reconstruction and development. 2002. xxviii, 357 pp.
13 OAKES, Leigh: Language and National Identity. Comparing France and Sweden. 2001. x, 305 pp.
12 OKITA, Toshie: Invisible Work. Bilingualism, language choice and childrearing in intermarried families. 2002. x, 275 pp.
11 HELLINGER, Marlis and Hadumod BUSSMANN (eds.): Gender Across Languages. The linguistic representation of women and men. Volume 3. 2003. xiv, 391 pp.
10 HELLINGER, Marlis and Hadumod BUSSMANN (eds.): Gender Across Languages. The linguistic representation of women and men. Volume 2. 2002. xiv, 349 pp.
9   HELLINGER, Marlis and Hadumod BUSSMANN (eds.): Gender Across Languages. The linguistic representation of women and men. Volume 1. 2001. xiv, 329 pp.
8   ARMSTRONG, Nigel R.: Social and Stylistic Variation in Spoken French. A comparative approach. 2001. x, 278 pp.
7   McCAFFERTY, Kevin: Ethnicity and Language Change. English in (London)Derry, Northern Ireland. 2001. xx, 244 pp.
6   RICENTO, Thomas (ed.): Ideology, Politics and Language Policies. Focus on English. 2000. x, 197 pp.
5   ANDREWS, David R.: Sociocultural Perspectives on Language Change in Diaspora. Soviet immigrants in the United States. 1999. xviii, 182 pp.
4   OWENS, Jonathan: Neighborhood and Ancestry. Variation in the spoken Arabic of Maiduguri, Nigeria. 1998. xiv, 390 pp.
3   LINELL, Per: Approaching Dialogue. Talk, interaction and contexts in dialogical perspectives. 1998. xvii, 322 pp.
2   KIBBEE, Douglas A. (ed.): Language Legislation and Linguistic Rights. Selected Proceedings of the Language Legislation and Linguistic Rights Conference, the University of Illinois at Urbana-Champaign, March, 1996. 1998. xvi, 415 pp.
1   PÜTZ, Martin (ed.): Language Choices. Conditions, constraints, and consequences. 1997. xxi, 430 pp.